MOSCOW DESPATCHES

MOSCOW DESPATCHES

Inside Cold War Russia

JOHN WATKINS

Edited and with an Introduction by
Dean Beeby and William Kaplan

James Lorimer & Company, Publishers
Toronto 1987

Copyright © 1987 by James Lorimer & Company, Publishers.
All rights reserved. No part of this book may be reproduced or transmitted in any form or by any means, electronic or mechanical, including photo-copying, or by any information storage or retrieval system, without permission in writing from the publisher.

Design and Cover Photo: Falcom Design & Communications

Photographs are reproduced courtesy of: Canapress Photo Service (1,12); UPI/Bettman Newsphotos (2-3); R.A.J. Phillips (4-10); Public Archives of Canada, PA 117601, PA 117617 (11, 13).

Canadian Cataloguing in Publication Data

Watkins, John 1903-1964

Moscow despatches

A selection from the official despatches written during Watkins' diplomatic postings in the Soviet Union.
ISBN 1-55028-028-7

1. Soviet Union - Social conditions - 1945-   - Sources.   2. Soviet Union - Politics and government - 1945-   - Sources.   3. Soviet Union - Descrip-tion and travel - 1945-1969.   I. Beeby, Dean.   II. Kaplan, William, 1957-   III. Canada. Embassy (Soviet Union).   IV. Title.

DK274.W38 1987   947.084'2   C87-094305-7

James Lorimer & Company, Publishers
Egerton Ryerson Memorial Building
35 Britain Street
Toronto, Ontario M5A 1R7

Printed and bound in Canada
5 4 3 2 1   87 88 89 90 91

"It sometimes feels here now as if the Russians had just re-read the old story of the contest between the wind and the sun to get the man to take his coat off and had decided for a change to turn on the full warmth of their renowned Slavic charm and see how it works. I don't see why we shouldn't take our coats off and be sociable but we must be careful to resist any wild impulses to divest ourselves of more of our attire than would be prudent or seemly."

John Watkins, Moscow 1955

For
Irina Efimov
and
Susan Krever

Contents

Acknowledgments

For their help in preparing the manuscript, our thanks go to John Holmes, George Ignatieff, Charles Ritchie, Peter Roberts, Maxwell Yalden, Geoffrey Pearson, Basil Robinson and R.A.J. Phillips, former colleagues of Watkins who kindly consented to one or more interviews. Ralph Reynolds, also a colleague, provided a delightful written account of his association with Watkins. Gaby Leger, a close friend of Watkins during his Paris retirement, offered personal reminiscences as did Naomi Roberts, Elizabeth Robinson, Arthur Andrew and Arnold Smith. Hugh Clark and his wife Phoebe McDougall-Clark patiently endured detailed questions about Watkins' youth, and gave one of us a tour of Watkins' old haunts in Norval and Norval Station. Several people we interviewed requested that they remain anonymous.

Chapman Pincher offered advice on research and sources, and Roger Bowen kindly forwarded a key primary source. Kenneth C. Brown, Co-ordinator of Access to Information and Privacy of the Department of External Affairs; P.E.J. Banning, Departmental Privacy and Access to Information Co-ordinator, Royal Canadian Mounted Police; and G.R.J. Montgomery, Chief of Information Access, Canadian Security Intelligence Service helped to remove obstacles that barred the way to the despatches. Additional assistance was provided by Emil P. Moschella, Chief of the Freedom of Information Section of the U.S. Department of Justice; and James R. Hall, Chief of the Freedom of Information Section of the U.S. Federal Bureau of Investigation.

Several staff members at the Department of External Affairs assisted the research, including Don Page, John Hilliker, Arthur Blanchette and

Dacre Cole of the History Directorate, and R. de Chantal, former director of the Academic Relations Division.

Marvin Rosenhek helped with the legal research. Adam Corelli and Betty Shewan provided historical information, and Michael Kaplan commented on an early draft. Robert Cherniak helped in the technical preparation of the manuscript. Generous financial assistance was provided by the University of Ottawa. Warm thanks also go to our agent, Stanley Colbert of the Colbert Agency, and to Heather Robertson and Curtis Fahey at James Lorimer & Company.

DB/WK, Ottawa, August 1987

Introduction

Thanksgiving in Quebec in 1964 was not the usual holiday weekend spent free from the cares of the world. The Queen's visit to Quebec City on Saturday had been punctuated by the protests of separatists just beginning to feel their power. British journalists were indignant that Canadian security had not kept the crowds at bay, and much of English Canada was confused and angry. Late on the holiday Monday came word that the Soviet Union had successfully orbited three men using technology said to be years ahead of the United States. ''Vostok'' was the first multi-passenger spaceship, a clear indication the Soviets had a head start in the race to the moon.

On that crisp, bright Monday, three men spent much of the day in a small room at a suburban Montreal Holiday Inn, also intent on the international scene. It had been a working weekend for the trio, but most of their business was done. At about a quarter to six, one of them flipped on the television to watch the Alouettes squeeze past the Blue Bombers 21-20. The three stared at the screen, welcoming the diversion, then left for the hotel dining room. The elderly one, sixty-one years old, had filet mignon, but with the onset of chest pains returned to his room to rest. He rejoined the others later, and after an hour of light reminiscing, reached for a cigarette. Before his fingers touched the package, he stopped, took a deep breath, threw his head back and died.

The dead man was John Benjamin Clark Watkins, a career diplomat and Canada's ambassador to the Soviet Union from 1954 to 1956. His companions were Leslie James Bennett and Harry Brandes, members of the Security Service, the counter-espionage and national security

division of the Royal Canadian Mounted Police. During almost a month
of interrogation, they had determined that the Soviet secret police had
successfully compromised Watkins by photographing him in a set-up
homosexual encounter during his posting in Moscow — and they had
just learned that the encounter was not the only one. Now they were
left with a delicate situation — a dead man at the conclusion of a
lengthy interrogation. After consulting their superiors, who in turn
informed Prime Minister Lester Pearson, they covered up the death
with the help of the local police. The circumstances of John Watkins'
demise were soon safely hidden in a few files in Ottawa, which remained
unopened for sixteen years.

The secret began to surface in 1980 with the publication of *Wilderness of Mirrors*, an account of Soviet espionage in the West. Author
David Martin revealed for the first time that Watkins had been the
target of homosexual blackmail by the Soviet secret police. He further
alleged Watkins was mocked for his homosexuality by Soviet leader
Nikita Khrushchev at a 1955 dinner for visiting Canadian External
Affairs Minister Lester Pearson. Martin also claimed Watkins died
while being questioned about the Russian trap by the Canadian Security
Service.

Public interest in the revelation began to well up the following year
with the March publication of *Their Trade is Treachery*, an exposé of
double agents by British journalist Chapman Pincher. Pincher's claim,
that Watkins died while being questioned in a Montreal hotel room,
caused a sensation in the press. One month later, in April 1981, Toronto
novelist Ian Adams added fuel to the fire with the second edition of
his controversial book, *S: Portrait of a Spy*. Adams had poked into
some dusty files and discovered that the Quebec coroner who signed
Watkins' death certificate did not realize who Watkins was and knew
nothing of the real circumstances of his death. There were calls in the
House of Commons for an inquest.

Further details about Watkins' entrapment soon began to emerge.
A two-part series written by a well-connected Ottawa journalist, John
Sawatsky, published in the Toronto *Star* and other papers in June 1981,
revealed how Watkins came to be in the suburban Montreal Holiday
Inn. While Canada's ambassador to the Soviet Union, Watkins made
a trip to several Central Asian Soviet republics. There, according to
Sawatsky's report of the RCMP interrogation, he had two homosexual
liaisons, one with an Uzbek poet (whom we identify as Nazir Akhimich
Akhundi), the other with a youth whose identity remains uncertain.
Although the Soviet secret police, the KGB, knew of the affair between

Watkins and Akhundi, they did not exploit it, apparently because Akhundi would not co-operate. More troublesome for Watkins was the second encounter. It also came to the attention of the KGB, who ordered the young man to send Watkins a postcard saying he would soon be in Moscow and would like to meet again. Watkins agreed. The relationship resumed and the two were secretly photographed in a homosexual encounter in a Moscow hotel room. With these photographs, the secret police tried to pressure Watkins into helping the Soviet side.

According to Sawatsky, Pincher and others, the successive defection of three KGB operatives brought details of the matter to the attention of Canadian authorities. First, in 1961, KGB Major Anatoli Golitsin came west with an incomplete account of the entrapment. Further details were added by Yuri Krotkov in 1963. And in 1964 KGB captain and long-time CIA double agent Yuri Nosenko defected and pinpointed John Watkins as the entrapped ambassador.

Watkins, in extremely poor health, was then roused from retirement in Paris and taken first to London, England, for questioning. There, during a break in the interrogation, he met his old friend, John Holmes, also a retired Canadian diplomat. Watkins, Holmes later recalled, admitted the circumstances which had led to his predicament and assured him he wanted to co-operate with the Security Service. The investigation next moved to Montreal. When Watkins died on Thanksgiving 1964 the interrogation was virtually complete. Bennett and Brandes established that Watkins had been compromised, but apparently concluded he had not betrayed Western secrets nor had he slanted Canadian policy toward the Kremlin.

News of these events brought pressure to bear on Ottawa to re-open the Watkins case, specifically to verify the circumstances of his death which clearly had not been reported fully to the Montreal coroner in 1964. In what some regarded as an effort to embarrass the RCMP, and thus the federal government, the Parti Québecois Minister of Justice ordered a coroner's inquest into Watkins' death, and the hearings got under way in October, 1981. Testimony by more than a dozen witnesses established that Watkins had co-operated fully with the Security Service investigation and had made every effort to clear his name. The inquest was told Bennett and Brandes had treated Watkins with respect and consideration throughout.

The coroner was also told that during a ten-day break in the interrogation, Watkins visited his cousins, Hugh and Phoebe Clark, in his home community of Norval Station, near Brampton, Ontario, and consulted his physician. Dr. Alec Capon advised Watkins to enter

hospital immediately but Watkins refused. Even the pleas of Phoebe
Clark to stay in Norval Station to rest failed to dissuade him. Watkins
was determined to return to Montreal to see the interrogation through.
Several days later he was dead. The coroner ruled in June 1982 that
Watkins died of natural causes, and carefully sidestepped the issue of
the manner in which the circumstances of his death had been concealed.

Word of Watkins' sad end was whispered in the corridors of the Department of External Affairs in the 1960s and 70s, long before the headlines
about his RCMP interrogation. And yet colleagues today say the revelations in no way diminish their fondness and respect for Watkins.
They recall him as a gentle, sociable man who took as much pleasure
in good food, fine wine and tobacco as he did in an evening of cultured
conversation. Often he would entertain guests at the piano, or discourse
at length about art, literature, philosophy and music — usually in the
same breath. Watkins was among the best-read at External Affairs,
and although his specialty was Scandinavian literature and history, he
could hold his own wherever the conversation might drift. Social gatherings often ended in the early morning hours with his renditions of
old Norwegian folk songs.

Watkins, his friends and colleagues recall, was an iconoclast who
had a gentle contempt for organized religion. Each year he would pick
out a new suit at Eaton's, and most of the time it was dusted with his
own cigarette ash. He was undisciplined in his personal habits — smok-
ing, drinking, eating — but had a highly disciplined mind. A collector
of modern art, especially avant garde Soviet painting, and a supporter
of starving artists, Watkins loaned all of his canvasses to friends and
colleagues. He had an excellent collection of Chagalls, for example,
along with several Russian triptychs acquired during his time in Moscow.
He was also a loyal correspondent, someone whose long, erudite letters
were stacked away in drawers by friends for re-reading someday.

But it is Watkins' despatches and letters from Moscow that colleagues
at External Affairs remember best about the man. Often during interviews for this book, former associates would gaze into the distance
recalling with a smile some particularly wry passage first read more
than 30 years ago. Even his RCMP interrogators took delight in reading
the hundreds of despatches and letters they had to study for evidence
of disloyalty. The documents acquired a reputation, years after they
were written, as literary gems that one read as much for pleasure as
for information.

After a request under the Access to Information Act, which took six months to satisfy, we had the despatches before us, and we too were struck by their literary qualities. An expression of the "belles lettres" tradition established in part by fellow diplomats Robert Ford and Charles Ritchie, the despatches provide intimate portraits of Soviet citizens with whom Watkins shared many evenings in animated conversation. They offer a glimpse of a vast country struggling, under the tyranny of Josef Stalin, to rebuild after the devastation of the Second World War. They detail the confusion in the Moscow diplomatic corps following Stalin's death. They catalogue the diversity of cultures in the Soviet Union, especially in the accounts of Watkins' trip to previously forbidden regions. And like a Greek tragedy, they chronicle Watkins' deepening involvement with two secret police operatives who eventually tried to blackmail him.

John Benjamin Clark Watkins, born 1902, was the first child of John Watkins and Jane Clark, who owned a farm near the small Grand Trunk railway depot of Norval Station, outside Brampton, Ontario. John and Jane had been raised on neighbouring farms, and attended the same Presbyterian church. Jane trained in Rhode Island to be a nurse, but returned to the Norval farm community where she forsook a nursing career to raise a family. In addition to John there were two daughters, Elizabeth (b. 1903) and Isabel (b. 1905).

Tragedy struck the young family in 1906. While the elder John was unloading a quarter of beef from a wagon, the horse stepped forward, causing a wheel to roll over his foot, crushing it. He contracted blood poisoning, and died soon after. Left with three small children and no money, Jane leased out the family farm and moved to a frame house at Norval Station where she supplemented her income by operating a coal business.

John (known throughout his youth as "Jack") was a slim boy without the stamina or physique for farm chores or sports. He pitched in at threshing time, and ran the coal business in his mother's rare absence, but his heart was in music, learning and long conversations. His father had been a choir director at the church, and John became organist. A chance encounter at a relative's farm set John upon a path he was to travel all his life. He struck up a friendship with a pair of Danish farmworkers, a boy and his uncle, neither of whom knew any English. John rapidly absorbed their Danish and acquired an early appreciation for Scandinavian culture.

At the University of Toronto, he studied French, German and Latin, as well as history, earning a Master's Degree by 1927. He paid for his schooling by working in the university library, and spent at least one summer, in 1925, working on the harvest in Western Canada. He also travelled to Europe in the late 1920s, to France, Holland and Denmark, where he acted as a guide and companion to the son of Heywood Broun, the syndicated columnist with the New York *World*. It was in Denmark that Watkins shed the name "Jack"; the Danes pronounced it "Yak" and he decided "Yon" was a more mellifluous corruption.

Watkins departed for the United States in 1930, first to New York City's Columbia University (1930-31 and 1933-34), then to Cornell University in September 1942 where he received a Ph.D. two years later. (His thesis was about the life and work of Danish dramatist and novelist Gustav Wied (1858-1914)). In 1930, Watkins joined the staff of the American-Scandinavian Foundation in New York where he spent more than a decade in progressively more senior positions, drinking in the intellectual life of New York. He returned to Canada during the Second World War, teaching first at Queen's University in Kingston, Ont., then at the Guelph Agricultural College. In 1944 he became an associate professor of English at the University of Manitoba in Winnipeg.

Throughout these years, tragedy continued to haunt Watkins' family. His sister Isabel had fought off a bout of tuberculosis in 1921, but a second attack in 1932 killed her. Elizabeth took a B.A. at the University of Toronto in 1928, and a diploma in Library Arts in 1934, but she could not find employment. Her mental health deteriorated, leading her through a succession of psychiatrists and mental institutions in southern Ontario until her death at a Woodstock home in 1954. Watkins' mother died of a stroke in 1942.

Far from cutting off his ties with Norval Station, the progressive loss of his family seemed to draw Watkins even closer to the community. He would visit his cousins there every summer for several weeks, and he retained ownership of the family farm and Norval Station house until his death. It was the only home Watkins would ever own. In conversation with strangers, he would present himself as a mere farm boy, and delighted in displaying a photograph of the substantial brick farmhouse that his mother had been raised in and where cousins put him up during every visit home.

Watkins joined the Department of External Affairs during its rapid expansion immediately after the Second World War. While at the University of Manitoba, he was invited by Hume Wrong, the assistant undersecretary of state for external affairs, to take the Canadian Foreign

Service Examination. By all accounts he only reluctantly agreed, and during the personal interview that followed the written test argued he was ill-suited to a diplomatic career. Despite his misgivings, Watkins was offered a position as a Foreign Service Officer (Grade 4), for the usual two-year probationary period, at a salary of $4,500. And so on September 3, 1946 he left the university for the Department of External Affairs, initially as First Secretary of the European Division, then as head of section. Exactly two years later, having passed probation, he was posted to Moscow as chargé d'affaires.

This rapid promotion was typical of the post-war period, as External Affairs established a presence in many foreign capitals befitting Canada's greater role in international relations. It was also a period during which the department remained an "old boy" club whose members sought out new recruits much like themselves. Hume Wrong and Lester Pearson were academics at the University of Toronto before joining the fledgling department in the 1920s. As a scholar with an international outlook, Watkins fit the mould well.

Watkins already knew some Russian on his arrival in Moscow in September 1948 and soon became fluent, setting himself apart from scores of unilingual Western diplomats in the Soviet capital. The Canadian mission was small — two secretaries and a military attaché. Demands on embassy personnel were not great. Much of their work consisted of summarizing Soviet press reports, analyzing speeches and making enquiries on behalf of Canadians who believed relatives were being held in the Soviet Union following the war. Moscow remained a closed society in which contacts with foreigners were strictly limited. Trips to Leningrad were permitted, but almost all other travel was forbidden. John Holmes, the departing chargé d'affaires in 1948, recalls the isolation as grim, yet intriguing because "you were close to the heart of the mystery." Watkins' task was to try to lift the veil.

For the first quarter century following the 1917 October revolution, Canada and the Soviet Union had no formal diplomatic relations whatsoever. The relationship was immediately strained in 1918, during the First World War, when some five hundred Canadian troops were dispatched at British request to Archangel and Murmansk to prevent the German army from capturing supplies that had been intended for the Czar's forces. After Vladimir Lenin made a separate peace with Germany in March 1918 (thereby freeing German troops for a renewed assault on the Western front), Leon Trotsky, the Soviet commissar for war, ordered the Murmansk Bolsheviks to oust the allied troops. A bitter battle ensued leaving two Canadians and ten British soldiers dead. Canada was also persuaded in 1918 to join a multi-national force in Siberia and sent approximately thirty-five hundred men to Vladivostok to protect war supplies and to safeguard the passage of a Czechoslovak legion to France. The last of the Canadian troops pulled out in June 1919.

Canadian interests in the Soviet Union were not wholly militaristic, however. Siberia, in particular, attracted attention as a potential market for Canadian goods, and by order-in-council Ottawa established a small trade mission in Vladivostok, headed by Dana Wilgress, a young Russophile whose experience would later prove invaluable to the Department of External Affairs. Wilgress' mission was to explore the possibility of selling Canadian equipment to help exploit Siberia's riches.

In March 1921, Britain signed a general trade agreement with Moscow and later that year Canada agreed to its terms. Wilgress and another Canadian, H.J. Mackie, were then transferred to the British mission in Moscow. The Soviet government reciprocated by setting up a trade office in Montreal. Much more significant, in 1924 Britain sent a note recognizing the Kremlin as the legitimate government of the lands contained in the Old Russian Empire. After a typically cautious delay of four months, Canadian Prime Minister William Lyon Mackenzie King informed the House of Commons that Canada was also extending *de jure* recognition to the Soviet regime.

A police raid in London, however, soon severed these tenuous diplomatic links. After uncovering evidence of Soviet espionage, a large British force broke into the Soviet trade office. The action turned up dozens of documents detailing espionage and subversive activities. The British government ended diplomatic contacts in May 1926. Canada dutifully followed suit and the Soviets closed their trade office in Montreal. A Labour minority government in Britain restored formal relations with the Soviet Union in June 1929, but Canada did not, preferring instead to let the British ambassador in Moscow look after the limited Canadian diplomatic interests.

The 1930s represent a low point in Canadian-Soviet relations. There were no direct diplomatic contacts and no lasting trade agreements or delegations. This decade-long vacuum has been attributed to the hostility French Canada and Slavic immigrants harboured toward the atheism and autocracy of the new Soviet state. But clearly it had as much to do with the Depression. The two economies were far from complementary, and Soviet leader Josef Stalin's plan for rapid industrialization required large exports of Soviet natural resources, a threat to Canada's markets. In February 1931, the Conservative government of Prime Minister R.B. Bennett slapped an embargo on a wide range of Soviet exports, including coal, woodpulp, lumber, asbestos and furs. However, the rise of Adolf Hitler brought the West and the Soviet Union closer together and, partly in recognition of the changed international scene, Mackenzie King (who returned to power in 1935) lifted the embargo in September 1936. By August 1939, a new trade deal had been signed conferring most-favoured-nation status on the Soviet Union, but the deal was nullified within days when Germany and Russia concluded a treaty of "Non-Aggression and Friendship." Less than a month after the pact was made Nazi and Soviet tanks invaded Poland, thereby launching the Second World War.

The Soviet Union watched from the sidelines during the ensuing "phony war" and the Nazi takeover of France, which began in May 1940. Then on June 22, 1941, Germany attacked its former ally, driving Stalin into the Western camp. Canada and the Soviet Union thus became allies, and the need for war planning led to formal diplomatic ties. Ottawa and Moscow signed a declaration in February 1942, agreeing to exchange diplomatic representatives. In September 1942, a Soviet mission was established in Ottawa. The Mackenzie King government chose Dana Wilgress as Canada's first diplomatic representative to the Soviet Union and in early 1943, Wilgress arrived in Kuibyshev, the Soviet wartime capital, where he held the rank of Minister Plenipotentiary. Later that year Nazi reverses made Moscow more secure and Wilgress along with his small staff moved to two buildings in the capital earlier vacated by the Danish legation. In early 1944, Wilgress presented his letter of accreditation as ambassador, and about the same time Canada extended its wartime Mutual Aid Agreement to include the Soviet Union. Planes, tanks, lumber and food were shipped to the U.S.S.R. before the agreement terminated in September 1945.

These strengthening Canadian-Soviet ties were shattered by the Gouzenko affair of 1945-46. Igor Gouzenko, a bright young cipher specialist working in the Soviet embassy in Ottawa, defected in the first week of September 1945. Gouzenko brought with him a sheaf of documents exposing a Canadian spy ring delivering intelligence to the Soviet Union. After an investigation, a dozen suspects were rounded up in early 1946 and brought to trial; eventually, a number were found guilty of betraying state secrets. The revelations not only rocked the Canadian government, but reverberated through all Western intelligence agencies and forced a re-evaluation of security.

The Soviet ambassador hurriedly left Ottawa in late 1945 when it became clear Gouzenko had defected. In Moscow, the Soviet guard around the Canadian embassy suddenly doubled and Wilgress reported a cooling off in relations. He was recalled in April 1947, and the mission was left for some years in the hands of a succession of chargés d'affaires, including John Holmes, John Watkins and Robert Ford.

The Gouzenko revelations had brought a chill to formal Canadian-Soviet relations, but Canadian policy toward the Soviet Union, formulated in large measure by the first ambassador, remained consistent. Wilgress' view, even after his departure from Moscow in 1947, helped shape Canadian policy toward the Soviet Union for more than a decade. In brief, Wilgress argued that the Soviets were opportunists who would enlarge their territory and sphere of influence as far as the allies would tolerate. He rejected the view that Soviet expansionism was the expression of a carefully devised plan. Rather, he believed Soviet leaders sought only to bolster their defences with a buffer zone of subject states in Eastern Europe. Wilgress' position was that the Soviets would not expand where Western resolve was clear, and so the West must pursue a tough, united stand against Soviet rapacity.

At the same time, Wilgress argued that the West must remain open to conciliatory gestures from the Kremlin — to hold them suspect, but not to dismiss them outright. In this respect Canadian thinking differed from that of leading British and American policy-makers who were less inclined to patience when the Soviets sent out diplomatic feelers. Never was there a suggestion that Canada act as a mediator between East and West. Ottawa was clearly and irrevocably in the British-American camp. Wilgress and other advisers, however, urged that Canada also pursue independent interests, a policy that fitted well with the government's desire to retain a distinct identity on the international stage. It was an enlightened policy, demanding diplomats of sensitivity and finesse at the Canadian mission in Moscow.

John Watkins seemed the ideal candidate. His entree into Soviet society was to be his intellect, his love of the arts and his penchant for refined conversation. He was to practise on a personal level the grander intent of Canada's policy toward the Soviet Union: where an opening presented itself, regard it with suspicion but explore the possibilities. There was something about his demeanour that invited the conversation of strangers. Watkins had a slightly stooped, innocent look, and presented a more rotund profile than in his youth — ''more like a kind of gnome'' than a diplomat, as colleague John Holmes remembers.

Even so, his three-year stint in Moscow from 1948 to 1951 lacked the wider social contacts Watkins would later enjoy as Canadian ambassador in the post-Stalin thaw. As chargé d'affaires, Watkins was able to form friendships with a handful of intellectuals, but these brought him no closer to the inner workings of the Kremlin. His despatches from this early period thus reflect the isolation from Soviet society that was typical of all Western missions.

The mission building itself had been acquired in haste during the last years of the war. Built by a pair of wealthy sugar-merchant brothers at the turn of the century, the imposing two-storey structure had self-contained dwellings on each level. The area was originally the mews for a large estate, as the address Stara-Konyushni or "street of the old stables" suggests. Watkins' apartment was on the upper floor, and above the garage in back was another small apartment that was used as an office. Soviet militiamen were stationed on the street in front to monitor who went in and out.

Once each week, a British courier would arrive to ferry a satchel of diplomatic correspondence to Ottawa, despatches addressed to the Secretary of State for External Affairs and letters to the undersecretary. Urgent correspondence would be sent by telegram after it was encoded by hand on a cypher machine. Watkins was aware, as were all embassy staff, that electronic eavesdropping devices were planted throughout the building. British and RCMP counter-intelligence officers had swept one room relatively clear of bugs, and it was there that some confidential conversations took place. Even in the "safe" room, though, Watkins would play a record or turn up the radio to confound any listening devices that had been missed. The U.S. ambassador in the 1950s, Charles Bohlen, writes in his memoirs that during renovations at the American embassy, workers found forty-three hidden microphones in what had been considered the most secure part of the building. All Western diplomats understood that the most confidential matters had to be discussed out in the street.

Toward the end of Watkins' first posting in Moscow he began to develop health problems that were to persist until the end of his life. His medical examination on joining the department had been perfunctory and failed to uncover heart and circulatory weaknesses. In January 1951, External Affairs announced Watkins was to return to Ottawa on sick leave, and would be replaced by Robert Ford as chargé d'affaires. Watkins arrived in mid-May, but before the year was out he was again posted overseas, this time to Norway. Oslo was a diplomatic back-water, but the appointment served several purposes: it gave Watkins a promotion for competent performance in Moscow, it played into his fascination with Scandinavian culture and it provided him with lighter diplomatic duties and thus an opportunity to rest.

The late 1940s and early 1950s, meanwhile, marked another low in Canadian-Soviet relations. The Gouzenko revelations were an early skirmish in what later came to be called the "cold war." The 1948 Communist seizure of power in Czechoslovakia, followed by the Berlin blockade, were viewed as unacceptable Soviet interference in European affairs. Western resolve to resist the widening of Moscow's sphere of influence was made formal in 1949 with the creation of the North Atlantic Treaty Organization (NATO) and later in the year, East and West bowed to the inevitable and carved Germany into two states. The cold war got decidedly warm in Asia when in June 1950, Soviet-backed forces swarmed over Korea's internal border in a surprise attack on the south. A United Nations' force under American direction was deployed and the front stabilized the following summer.

The international chill seemed impenetrable until Soviet authorities revealed the death of Stalin, on March 6, 1953. After three days of silence at the Kremlin, the Soviet leadership announced that Georgi Malenkov had assumed the posts of Communist Party secretary and prime minister. The succession appeared complete, but by mid-March Malenkov had resigned his party stewardship in favour of Nikita Khrushchev. Malenkov and Khrushchev appeared to be in competition, and for the next two years the guessing game in the Moscow diplomatic corps was just who would emerge victorious.

Rumours of intrigue in the Kremlin soon began to surface. A short time before Stalin's death, nine doctors were accused of having plotted the 1948 death of Andrei Zhdanov, Stalin's chief lieutenant and heir apparent. The supposed "assassination" was said to have been followed by a 1949 purge of the Leningrad party organization, which had been Zhdanov's stronghold. Details of the purge (referred to cryptically as the "Leningrad Affair" in the Soviet press) were unclear, but suspicions soon fell on Lavrenti Beria, head of the Soviet secret police. Beria was first accused of insufficient vigilance, then of attempting to seize power, and in December 1953 it was announced that he and six followers had been executed.

Beria's downfall spawned new speculation about where the real power lay in the Kremlin. Malenkov had aligned himself with Beria in advocating relaxed industrial and agricultural policies, and the execution cast a long shadow over the new prime minister. Khrushchev, by contrast, advocated increasing heavy industry at the expense of consumer goods. Malenkov was eventually to resign, admit his "mistakes" in agricultural policy and renounce his emphasis on production of consumer goods. He would be replaced in 1955 by Nikolai Bulganin, a Politburo member since 1948. But before Malenkov was so ignominiously removed from power, he made some diplomatic overtures that reverberated around the world.

Malenkov expressed a new willingness to resolve points of conflict with the West, and by the summer of 1953 an armistice was signed in Korea. In November 1953, the Soviet Union appointed an ambassador to Ottawa, Dimitri Chuvakhin. The re-appointment of an ambassador was a clear signal, and the Department of External Affairs was quick to exploit the apparent easing of tensions by appointing a Canadian ambassador to Moscow. In late December 1953, there was speculation in the press that Watkins had become the leading candidate, and on January 21, 1954 it was made official: John Watkins was to be Canada's first peace-time ambassador to the Soviet Union.

There is no evidence that any security concerns were expressed about Watkins at the time of his appointment. His homosexuality was virtually unknown and, in any case, the sexual conduct of civil servants was not yet a major preoccupation in the West. In the late 1940s civil servants swore the Official Secrets Act oath and security investigations were made into the backgrounds of hundreds of personnel in sensitive positions. But the RCMP and other Western security organizations focussed on ideological converts to Communism who became spies out of a sense of higher purpose, not on subjects of potential sexual blackmail. Indeed, it was not until the mid-1950s that it become clear in the West that the Soviet secret police relied heavily on sexual entrapment to recruit spies. The RCMP Security Service launched a purge of homosexuals in the civil service during the 1950s and 1960s, but by that time Watkins was a valued and trusted employee at External Affairs.

Curiously, as early as August 1951, Watkins' loyalty to the West had come under scrutiny in the United States when the FBI began its own investigation of his past. Parts of the bureau's file on Watkins that have been released under the U.S. Freedom of Information Act make no reference to homosexuality, focussing instead on Watkins' ideological orientation. FBI interviews with associates in Albany, Buffalo, Boston, New York and Chicago all suggested Watkins was a loyal, trustworthy person. Typical were the following comments: ". . . absolutely no suspicions regarding Watkins' loyalty and Watkins' whole outlook on life seems to be pointed in the opposite direction of Communism . . . a person of good loyalty, character and associates . . . had no reason to doubt his loyalty, he believes him to be a person who could be entrusted with confidential information without any hesitancy.''

The investigation was likely sparked by secret testimony from Elizabeth Bentley before a U.S. Congressional committee in 1949 and by her continuing assistance to the FBI in the early 1950s. Bentley, who spied for the Soviet Union in New York, recanted and began to identify former associates to U.S. authorities. Among those she exposed was Vladimir Kazakevich, an academic whose intelligence gathering for the Soviets was to be documented over the years in a 400-page FBI file. Watkins knew Kazakevich from their student days at Columbia University, and his loyalty might have been called into question through this association. Whatever the reason, however, the FBI investigation of Watkins appears to have stalled soon after it began, although the file remained open until his death in 1964.

The newly-appointed ambassador arrived at the Canadian mission on March 3, 1954 during the thickest snowstorm of the winter. There the departing head of mission, Robert Ford, introduced Watkins to the staff and brought him up to date on developments at the embassy. The mission now employed ten Canadians and nine locally hired personnel. More taxing than the administrative responsibilities of running the mission, however, was the need to assess the fluid political situation. Watkins' task was onerous — to pick through snippets of information emerging from the Kremlin, to distinguish rumour from fact and to report on the latter to his superiors in Ottawa.

Although it was crucial to have reliable information, even seasoned diplomats found the prospect daunting. The dean of Western representatives in Moscow during the period, British Ambassador Sir William Hayter, wrote in his memoirs: ''After a year in Moscow, I discussed, in a despatch to the Foreign Office, the quite genuine question whether it was worth maintaining an Embassy in Moscow at all.'' As Hayter explained to Whitehall, there were only three reasons for being in the Soviet capital: experience of the country, information about Soviet conditions and the symbolic value of an embassy.

Back home, Canadians were curious about the Soviet state, especially in light of the dire threat to peace that many Western politicans said it posed, but Watkins' second sojourn in Moscow attracted little media attention. Indeed, there was but a trickle of genuine news to satisfy readers' appetites. One minor diplomatic incident that occurred early in Watkins' tenure, though, was reported widely in the press. In October 1954, the Burmese ambassador, Maung Ohn, invited seven Western ambassadors, including Watkins, to a dinner party also attended by the Chinese and East German heads of mission. Neither East Germany nor China had been recognized by the West, and accordingly, Western diplomats could not sit at the same table with them. The Western diplomats walked out — a potential offence to Soviet Foreign Minister Viacheslav Molotov who also attended. The incident, whether an ill-advised attempt to bridge the gap between East and West or an effort to embarrass Western diplomats, was seized upon by the Western press. Watkins' despatch about the incident, included in this collection, details the somewhat comic scrambling to contain the diplomatic damage.

International exchanges, also a feature of the early post-Stalin thaw, were reported fully on both sides of the Iron Curtain. In the summer of 1955, Watkins accompanied Canada's fisheries minister, James Sinclair, for part of his tour of the Soviet Union. Later he joined a group of Soviet farm experts on a visit to Canada in August and September, 1955. Other exchanges took place, but the most important during Watkins' Moscow posting was the October 1955 visit of Canada's Secretary of State for External Affairs, Lester B. Pearson.

Pearson was the first Western foreign minister to travel to the Soviet Union since the creation of NATO. His visit, highlighted by a celebrated drinking session at Khrushchev's "dacha" (cottage) in the Crimea, was more than just a public relations exercise. It led to a three-year trade agreement in February, 1956 that sent about 1.5 million tons of wheat to the Soviet Union at world prices; it established that Khrushchev was in charge at the Kremlin; and it finally confirmed that the Soviets were keen to broaden contacts with the West. This last development, though, was already well known to External Affairs in Ottawa; the undersecretary had been reading about it every week in Watkins' Moscow despatches and letters. Indeed, the new ambassador had forged links with the Kremlin that were unique among Western representatives in the Soviet capital.

This collection of Watkins' despatches opens with several numbered letters written during his tenure as chargé d'affaires (1948-51) in the last years of Stalin's iron rule. At this time, Watkins re-established contact with Vladimir and Emily Kazakevich, the Marxist academics he had known in the United States. Kazakevich and his wife settled in Moscow in 1949, where Vladimir took a job at the Institute of Economics. They were perhaps Watkins' closest Moscow friends and the three often spent days together visiting museums and galleries, and evenings over leisurely meals. Watkins' reports of time spent with Vladimir and Emily include enchanting discussions of living conditions and popular culture. The Kazakeviches were eager to obtain from Watkins information about the West, and about himself, most of which was likely relayed to Soviet authorities.

The heart of this collection is Watkins' account of his trip to the once-forbidden Central Asian Soviet republics during his second Moscow posting. From the end of the Second World War, the region had been a potential battleground as the Soviets sought to secure their southern flank with a buffer similar to Eastern Europe. Soviet troops remained in Iran until well after the close of hostilities, and only in the post-Stalin thaw was a trickle of Westerners allowed through. Watkins was one of the first Westerners to visit and report on conditions in the mysterious underbelly of the Soviet empire.

The despatches detailing this trip reveal the presence of KGB agents. Watkins, who travelled alone, must have known he was never far from watchful eyes. Yet it was during this tour that he apparently let down his guard and had the two homosexual encounters that would haunt him for years. Soon after his return to Moscow, Watkins' circle of friends began to widen as the secret police initiated a sophisticated plot to bring him to the Soviet side. Read carefully, and with the advantage of hindsight, the despatches and letters from that point forward reveal a secret police operation of Byzantine proportions against a foreign diplomat.

The web is very thick indeed, and not always clear, but at its centre is the figure of Alexei Gorbunov, or "Alyosha." He was, in fact, Oleg Gribanov, a high-ranking KGB officer, assigned to the Watkins case, who worked undercover at the Institute of History. (Gribanov's career has been documented in John Barron's authoritative *KGB: The Secret Work of Secret Agents*). "Alyosha" became a close acquaintance of Watkins, in concert with other KGB operatives and conscripts. Among these was Anatoly Nikitin, who presented himself as a professor of history, but who has been identified by Barron and others as Anatoly Gorsky (or Gorski), one of Gribanov's senior officials and who worked under the same cover as late as the mid-1970s.

With Nikitin in tow, Watkins spent a weekend at "Alyosha's" dacha in the Crimea. The three also went to Moscow restaurants frequently, and sometimes retired to the Canadian Embassy for long evening discussions. Gradually, Watkins came to believe that "Alyosha" was Khrushchev's right-hand man and he eagerly reported to Ottawa what he considered to be the fruits of a highly fertile contact. Indeed, "Alyosha" was instrumental in assuring that the Pearson visit in 1955 included a visit with Khrushchev, and that negotiations on a wheat deal got off the ground. "Alyosha" was a valuable acquaintance on a purely diplomatic level, and was soon well known at External Affairs in Ottawa. Indeed, Watkins' stature as a diplomat rose in tandem with the increased flow of information from the mysterious academic.

"Alyosha's" camaraderie also had sinister intent. According to the Sawatsky interrogation account, it was "Alyosha" who told Watkins — shortly before his return to Ottawa — about the photographs of the homosexual liaison with the youth in the Moscow hotel room. Assuming the role of friend and protector, "Alyosha" said he would hold off the KGB if only Watkins would "be friendly to Chuvakhin," that is, if he would ensure that Canadian policy accommodated Soviet goals. This delicate approach to Watkins skirted the danger of the ambassador confessing everything to his superiors in Ottawa, something that could damage détente with the West, just as the Gouzenko affair soured relations for many years.

Although the growing relationship with "Alyosha" and Nikitin dominates the despatches from late 1954 on, Watkins also reports on events of international significance, none more so than the Twentieth Communist Party Congress in early 1956 during which Khrushchev denounced Stalin in a speech to a closed session. The address — which attacked Stalin's war record, his purges of the army and his brutality — stands as a milestone in the evolution of the Soviet state. For a generation, unbridled terror reigned in the Soviet Union; now, three years after Stalin's death, Khrushchev challenged that record and intimated the advent of a more humane state. It is now clear that the speech was not the death-knell of totalitarianism, but rather a high-water mark (until recently) of liberalizing trends in the Soviet Union. But at the time, the revelations kindled hope in the West that the intransigence of the Stalin years was giving way to an era of dialogue.

Watkins was not personally to witness the aftermath. On April 3, 1956, Lester Pearson announced the ambassador was to return to Canada to take up duties as assistant undersecretary. That an ambassadorial posting should end after only two years is odd. It is known Watkins wrote to External Affairs in 1955 for an estimate of his pension should he retire immediately. And after word of his entrapment became known at External Affairs, there were those who wondered whether this request and the shortened posting had something to do with the attempted KGB blackmail.

After two years in Ottawa, Watkins was appointed ambassador to Denmark, a quiet post to ease the strain on his heart. But his health continued to decline. He had by now developed diabetes and spent Christmas of 1959 bedridden at a Copenhagen hospital with a nosebleed that would not stop. In 1960, Watkins returned to Ottawa, quite unwell and taking heart medication regularly. Lengthy medical leaves did not improve his health and on July 25, 1963, he officially retired, a few months before his 61st birthday. Before leaving Ottawa for retirement in France, Watkins distributed his valuable library of Russian and Scandinavian books to several Canadian universities and gave his collection of Picassos, Chagalls and Russian avant garde paintings to many friends for safekeeping.

Watkins lived quietly in the Lennox Hotel on the Left Bank in Paris, a city he loved. Most of his neighbours were students, and he liked to remind guests that James Joyce once lived there. He became a patron and friend of many unknown artists, including Basil Rakoczi, Maurice Brasser and Bernard Citroën (a relative of the car manufacturer), buying their work and supplying them with food and drink. Often Watkins was a dinner guest of Jules and Gaby Leger at the Canadian Embassy. (Leger later became Governor General of Canada, 1974-79.) In May, he entertained his cousins Hugh and Phoebe Clark in the French capital, then took them on a motor tour of Europe. But the visit was a strain, and Watkins had his first heart attack that summer. The Legers helped nurse their old friend back to health at their villa in Fontainebleau, southeast of Paris. He moved into a small flat in Montparnasse in September, and just as he got back on his feet again, two men from the Security Service came calling.

The Canadian Security Intelligence Service (CSIS), the successor to the RCMP Security Service, has refused to release the bulk of the Watkins interrogation report. However, Sawatsky's account of the interrogation, based on unidentified sources, has withstood numerous tests of accuracy. Although we found minor variations in other sources (including the despatches and the 1980-81 Quebec coroner's inquest), the narrative in *For Services Rendered* stands as the most authoritative description yet to find its way into print. It has been confirmed by sources in CSIS, by numerous interviews, and by documents — including parts of the interrogation report — obtained under the Access to

Information Act. Both CSIS and Department of External Affairs files reveal that the Security Service contacted Watkins via Jules Leger, who reluctantly agreed to co-operate, and then only after the interrogation had been approved at the highest levels of the Department of External Affairs.

During the interrogation, Watkins and the Security Service agents developed a relationship based on mutual respect. In an interview seventeen years after Watkins' death, Bennett told a reporter: "I'm convinced in my own mind ..., and I've been convinced since talking to him over that period of time and examining the information on defection in retrospect, that he was never a traitor, that he obviously had been caught in homosexual compromise and the Russians had tried very skilfully to exploit this to their advantage but that they had really been totally unsuccessful."

Bennett continued: "I think it's most likely that this blackmail attempt, although skilfully done, could have rebounded to their disadvantage. I think he became more firmly entrenched against the Soviet regime than he might otherwise have been if they hadn't made that play at him." Watkins is quoted by Brandes as saying: "You can question my judgment but not my loyalty." Such, apparently, was the substance of the report Bennett and Brandes delivered to their superiors in Ottawa. It is worth noting that Bennett himself later came under suspicion of being a Soviet mole, and was forced to resign from the Security Service. However, there is no evidence to suggest the Security Service investigation of Watkins was anything but thorough and complete, and no evidence has yet surfaced to suggest Watkins was a traitor. Some evidence points in the opposite direction. As assistant undersecretary following his return from Moscow, Watkins was faced with a request from the Soviet Union to increase the size of its mission in Canada, likely to broaden espionage activities. Watkins turned down the request. However, until key government documents are released, including the full interrogation report, questions about Watkins' loyalty will continue to be raised.

The day after Thanksgiving 1964, the City of Montreal police telephoned Phoebe Clark and asked what should be done with Watkins. Was there an accident, she asked in alarm? No, no, he's dead, was the abrupt reply.

The Clarks arranged to have the body brought home. Watkins' funeral at the Norval Presbyterian Church attracted a handful of old acquaintances from the Department of External Affairs. Afterward, friends and family drove over to the big brick farmhouse that John always considered home, and, with drinks served, the afternoon turned into an old-fashioned Irish wake. Everyone had an anecdote to share about John. Because Watkins never had a permanent place in which to hang his collection of paintings, he had loaned them to friends and with his death they became gifts and mementoes.

Watkins' body was cremated, according to his wishes, and the ashes are interred in the family plot in Norval alongside his parents and two sisters. Watkins' last will and testament gave a small part of his property and possessions to his faithful cousins Hugh and Phoebe Clark. The bulk of the estate, though, was a gift to his fellow Canadians in the form of a bequest to the Canada Council.

Maxwell Yalden, then with the Canadian embassy in Paris, cleaned out Watkins' flat. It was very spare and when he told the Clarks in Norval about the few possessions, they asked Yalden to distribute them among John's many friends.

Watkins' despatches are reproduced here in their original form. Where significant amounts of material have been omitted, this has been indicated by the use of ellipses and an extra line-space. Obvious typographical mistakes have been corrected and an effort has been made to standardize the spelling of proper names.

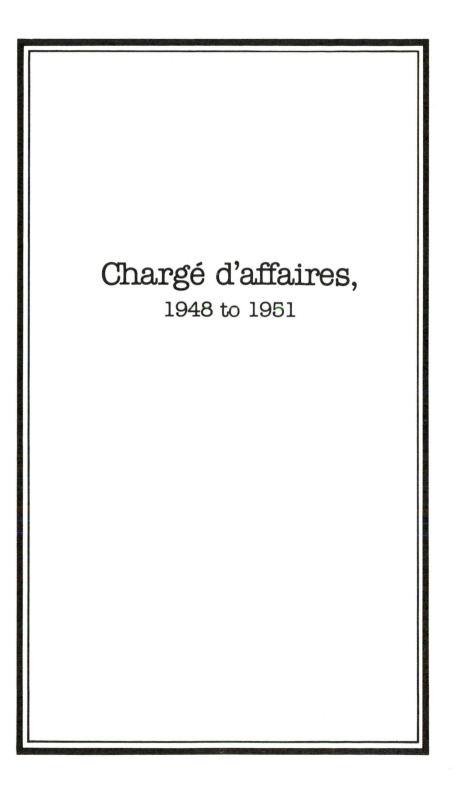

Chargé d'affaires,

1948 to 1951

The secrets of the Kremlin have always been well hidden from Western diplomats, no more so than during the one-man rule of Joseph Stalin from 1927 to 1953 (in his despatches, Watkins refers to Joseph Stalin, then the commonly accepted spelling of the name). One key source was the press corps in Moscow, which occasionally happened upon useful information. U.S. Ambassador Charles Bohlen, for instance, met with journalists at least once a week, and played poker with them regularly to soak up the latest gossip. Sometimes reporters in the capital stumbled onto significant stories. Ralph Parker (described below) apparently broke the story of Khrushchev's denunciation of Stalin at the Twentieth Party Congress in a despatch to the London Daily Worker. *At the same time, reporters were as desperate for information as diplomats and eagerly sought out contacts with them. However, as the following comments make clear, many reporters were suspected of ulterior motives and it was essential to know their backgrounds to avoid being baited. In one of Watkins' earliest communications with Ottawa, he attempts to catalogue the reliability of his journalist associates.*

— December 10, 1948 (Letter 574) —

… The representatives of the foreign press in Moscow have deteriorated in numbers and, to some extent, in quality since the days of the war.… At the present time there is only one representative of the United Kingdom press accredited to Moscow and he has been absent from the country for a long period on leave. There are now no outstanding Western writers here. I shall list the most important representatives of the foreign press and add a few personal comments on each of them.…

Eddy Gilmore: Associated Press. Mr. Gilmore has been in Moscow longer than most of the foreign correspondents now here. He has a nose for facts, particularly for out-of-the-way information, and is very interested in Soviet personalities. I do not think that he is capable of penetrating assessments of broad Soviet problems. He has the reputation of being a lone wolf and has made enemies among other correspondents and members of the diplomatic corps. He is right-wing, loathes the Soviet system and criticizes it as much as he can in view of his marriage to a Soviet citizen. He mixes with Soviet citizens more than most correspondents and knows many of them because of his long stay here and because of his wife's connections.

Edmund Stevens: Christian Science Monitor. Mr. Stevens is another old-timer who has had his Moscow post since the middle of the War. Opinion is divided on his worth but I personally do not consider him to be a particularly intelligent observer. He wrote a book about wartime Moscow which is very thin.[1] He has considerable resources of factual information about the Soviet Union and knows a great deal about Soviet personalities, but I do not think that he is capable of first-rate assessments of the Soviet system. He married a Russian citizen who now possesses a United States passport and who, up to the present, has had no difficulty in entering and leaving the country.

Henry Shapiro: United Press. Mr. Shapiro might be described as a left-wing intellectual who is disgruntled with modern society, but there is little doubt where his loyalties lie in a conflict between the United States and the Soviet Union. He has been in the Soviet Union for thirteen years in all and has a better factual knowledge of the country's revolutionary history than any other correspondent here. He attaches himself to the United States Ambassador and works closely with the United States Embassy. He is not popular with his colleagues or in the diplomatic corps. He is now living with a Russian woman....

Ralph Parker: As you know, Mr. Parker's connections with the Western press are mysterious and indefinite. He is — or was — a man of considerable intelligence with an excellent knowledge of the Soviet Union. During the War he was a correspondent for the London *Times* from which he was dismissed for his lack of objectivity. He was dismissed from the staff of the *News Chronicle* for the same reason. During the past year he has written for a Czechoslovakian, a Swedish and an Egyptian paper and is said to be working on another book. Mr. Parker is completely under the influence of the Russian woman with whom he lives and it is rumored that the nature of his writing in recent years is directly attributable to some form of blackmail which his mistress, or her M.V.D.[2] employers, are holding against him. His relations with western missions have been cool for a long time and his public statements at the time of the Czechoslovakian coup were all that were needed to make him officially and completely *persona non grata* with the United Kingdom Embassy. His writings now appear occasionally in the *Daily Worker*. It is rumored that he is accredited to this paper but we have yet to confirm this connection.

Tatiana Sofiane: Time and Life. Mr. Luce has chosen as his *pro tem* representative in Moscow an unusual figure. She is a survivor of the Czarist aristocracy who first became associated with westerners when she worked with American engineers during the thirties. When the United States agreed to enter into diplomatic relations but had not yet established an Embassy, she is said to have been unofficially in charge of United States interests here. During the purge her husband fell into disfavour, and it is generally supposed that he was shot. She herself was in prison for a long time. For many years past she has been closely associated with the foreign correspondents or with the United States Embassy. Considering her citizenship she is at times remarkably candid about the Soviet Union. As far as I know, there is no immediate prospect of a new *Time - Life* correspondent and hence I expect that she will fill this role for some time....

Jean Naud: France Press. Mr. Naud, like other French correspondents who have gone before him, is an unsavoury character. If he is not a member of the Communist Party he is so near it that it is a distinction without a difference. He is said to have been deeply involved in black market activities and his personal conduct at social functions is unpleasant. Insofar as he exerts influence on his colleagues, it is a bad influence. He has a Russian wife....

I regret that this may seem a depressing chronicle. I may have been harsh but I have discussed these men with my colleagues in other missions, and there is little disagreement about the characters of most of the representatives of the foreign press.

The United Kingdom Embassy is unhappy about the present situation. On the one hand, it is reluctant to throw fuel into the Soviet propaganda machine by having more correspondents in Moscow to turn out publicity for the Soviet censorship. On the other hand, the United Kingdom Embassy regrets that so few British journalists have an opportunity to get experience in Moscow. A number of British newspapers have endeavoured to send men here within the past two years but the arrangements have in all cases broken down either because of the failure to obtain Soviet visas and accreditations or because of the rising costs of keeping a representative in Moscow.

One of the few issues on which Soviet and American delegates at the United Nations agreed was the partition of Palestine and the creation of the State of Israel, in May, 1948. Yet a bare seven months later, the Soviet Union began a fierce anti-Semitic

campaign that persisted until Stalin's death in 1953. As Watkins
reported in early 1949, the campaign was launched as a purge
of foreign influence in the arts. The ostensible targets were
"homeless cosmopolitan double-dealers and their lickspittles,"
which in the parlance of the Kremlin was a clear reference to
Jews. Yet as Watkins notes, with the emergence of Israel, Jews
no longer were homeless and it would appear many Soviet Jews
applied to emigrate to the new homeland. Watkins here probes
the ideological and practical problems Israel posed for the Krem-
lin. In a subsequent despatch (see February 1, 1955, below),
Watkins describes an encounter with some Soviet Jews very inter-
ested in the establishment of the State of Israel.

— March 3, 1949 (Letter 143) —

... A member of the Israeli Legation in Moscow recently remarked to
a member of my staff that it was foolish to think of anti-Semitism as
a symptom of decadent capitalism: it had its own causes and it was
undoubtedly present in the Soviet Union as everywhere that Jews are
found (presumably with the exception of Israel). The current attacks
on Jews, however, stem from more than racial dislike; they have their
sources in ideological incompatibility. It is the ideological watchdogs
who have given the push, and it is the Soviet citizens who dislike Jews
who added to the movement against them. The Jewish intellectual has
not fitted himself into the rigid Soviet mould. He has long and deep
traditions of internationalism in culture (or, if you wish, cosmopoli-
tanism). His position is a constant potential threat to the moulding of
the arts in a completely Soviet pattern, and to the insulation of Soviet
intellectuals from the baneful influence of the outside world. The
contradictions in the character of the Soviet Jewish intellectual have
been sharpened by the creation of his physical homeland. It is possible
that the Soviet authorities are attacking the homeless cosmopolitans
because they are no longer, in fact, homeless. Concern over ideological
deviation may extend to fear of questionable political loyalty in the
event of international conflict.

It is necessary to be cautious in linking this manifestation of anti-
Semitism with Soviet foreign policy, but I think that the connection
is no doubt there. As I have reported in separate despatches, the Soviet
Government may now be a little uneasy about its immediate and strong
diplomatic support of Israel, for there are many reasons to make the
close association of the two states difficult. Zionism is hateful to

Communism. That the growing caution of the Kremlin in its relations with Israel and its softening towards the Arab world should come at the same time as the Kremlin is stamping out internationalist (i.e. anti-Soviet) tendencies of Jews at home, seems more than coincidence. From the beginning of the Israeli state, the Soviet press has taken pains to warn Soviet citizens that they are happier here than in warmer climes, and that their task is to build socialism, or Communism, where they live. The Ministry of Internal Affairs has taken pains to ensure that the Israeli Legation in Moscow is not troubled by the visits of Jews who might be interested in meeting their countrymen from abroad. The Soviet authorities have always been alive to the implications of Jewish internationalism; it has now decided to attack it directly, and, incidentally, to open the door to the closet where the skeleton of ordinary reactionary racialism has been hanging....

— March 17, 1949 (Letter 163) —

[With evident bemusement, Watkins discusses an element of Soviet revisionism designed to depict Russia as the cradle of modern science and technology.]

... The Soviet press goes back to the eleventh century to illustrate the superiority of the Russian mind over the Anglo-Saxon. In 1066, it is said, the benighted Anglo-Saxons tried in vain to beat off the Norman invaders with stone axes, while at the same period, as is well known, the Russian princes were hacking each other with iron weapons. Revelations like this, or the [Russian] discovery of radio or penicillin, are no doubt meant to bring a glow of pride to the Soviet citizen, or at any rate to the Russian. By and large, it is only within the past year that most Russian inventions have been drawn to public attention. In many cases the inventions "have just been discovered in hitherto unknown papers brought to light in the archives of the Academy of Sciences."

Watkins and his associate at the Canadian mission, Robert Phillips, attended a session of the Supreme Soviet on March 3, 1949, at which they saw Stalin at close range for the first time. Under the Soviet Constitution, the Supreme Soviet is the country's highest legislative body. It consists of two chambers, the Soviet of the Union, whose delegates are elected on the basis of population, and the Soviet of Nationalities, with seats allocated to represent the various Soviet republics and regions. As the follow-

ing letter illustrates, senior diplomats from the West had few opportunities even to view Stalin, much less meet with him.

— March 18, 1949 (Letter 162) —

...As you know, these meetings have little political significance and with the exception of the budget statement little important business is done at them. Nevertheless, since I had an opportunity of attending the sessions this year, it may be of some interest if I provide you with a brief description of the Soviet trappings of democracy....

For the past two years members of the diplomatic corps have not been invited to attend the sessions of the Supreme Soviet. A few weeks before this year's session was due to begin, we sent a note to the Ministry saying that Mr. [Robert] Phillips and I wished to attend. On the opening day we received passes which allowed us to observe all of the sessions....

... Stalin, making one of his rare materializations at close range, was accompanied by Molotov, Beria, Malenkov, Mikoyan, Kaganovich, Suslov, Ponomarenko, Bulganin, Kosigyin, Voroshilov, Shvernik, as well as ministers not in the Politburo.... Mr. Phillips observed Mr. Stalin with binoculars at fairly close range for about fifteen minutes before being caught by an unsavoury plain-clothesman. I then examined the leader through the glasses but it was not long until I too was put in my place. (Binoculars were permitted in the afternoon but not in the evening when Stalin and other leading lights were present.) Neither of us had seen Stalin at close range before and we were both surprised at his healthy appearance. He was not as short as I expected and seemed little or no shorter than the average Russian or Georgian with whom he entered the hall. He wore an immaculate light grey uniform. His face was tanned. (Even binoculars did not reveal whether or not he used make-up.) His hair was very light grey. He remained in the hall for only about twenty minutes during which time he sat unostentatiously in the centre of the back row of the stage. During this time he committed no significant acts except to scratch his right ear. In the course of the Minister of Finance's speech there was a reference to the great Stalin at which the hall arose and applauded politely. Stalin also rose and applauded. A few minutes later he slipped out and did not return....

It is interesting to speculate on whom the Party expects to fool by this solemn farce. They probably fool a good many people, including most of the delegates themselves. The deputies are treated as important people while in Moscow and probably most have a great sense of responsibility as the makers of the country's laws. To them there is probably nothing unusual in the limitations of their power for they have known nothing else. They, therefore, regard the institution of which they are a part as an unparalleled gift to the people from the great and beneficent Stalin.

I have wondered if it would be possible to interest the Canadian press in poking fun at this sacred Soviet institution. During the sessions of our own House it should not be difficult to draw telling comparisons on the nature of the Soviet and Canadian parliamentary systems. There are surely few show pieces of Soviet propaganda which are so vulnerable to attack as the Supreme Soviet.

— May 2, 1949 (Letter 239) —

[Watkins' first observation of a May Day parade focussed in large part on the health of Stalin.]

... Rumours of the deplorable state of Stalin's health have been numerous. Just recently the Alsop brothers have established in their *Herald-Tribune* column the "fact" that in late 1948 he suffered no fewer than four apoplectic strokes. His ascent up the two flights of stairs to the reviewing stand on Lenin's tomb was therefore avidly scanned from the diplomatic cloister at its base. Nimble was the word for it. At the half-way point he paused, half turned to face in our direction, and flicked his august wrist in what we think may have been intended as a collective greeting. Whether it was meant for us or not, it is said to be a new departure. He then proceeded just as nimbly to the top and from that point on our view of him was confined to the tip of his ears and the peak of his cap, neither of which, I regret to report, was any more revealing than his expression. His disintegration, which can presumably not be indefinitely delayed, seems to be depressingly gradual. The possibility of a double à la Hitler has been suggested, but nobody seems to believe in it. His relatively dignified exterior would probably be more difficult to counterfeit successfully than Hitler's opéra bouffe façade, and the United Kingdom Minister assures us that nobody who had seen and talked with him on the Berlin question last August could credit the current rumours about his health; there was no indication then of declining mental powers and although not youthful he

was far from decrepit physically. Not to seem overly pessimistic, I
might add that the Greek Chargé knows a Greek resident of Moscow
who knows a Spaniard who knows a Spanish woman married to a
Russian doctor who says that Stalin's physician has forbidden him to
smoke his pipe on account of a serious heart condition. An American
woman who saw a May Day parade here some fifteen years ago noted
that this time he had not retired around the corner of the tomb for a
few puffs on his corn-cob as he had done then; but of course in those
days he used to stay on the reviewing stand saluting and waving until
the last spontaneous demonstrator had passed by. Yesterday he left
about ten minutes after the military parade was over, but is reported
to have appeared again later in the day....

— July 29, 1949 (Letter 372) —

... I am enclosing the ... Soviet Statistical Administration report on
the fulfilment of the five-year plan during the second quarter of 1949.
As usual the plan is reported to have been fulfilled in spite of minor
failures for particular commodities. The most outstanding achievement
reported in the economy of the workers' paradise is that the production
of champagne in this period is 453 percent of the production in the
second quarter of 1948. The percentage for beer, on the same basis,
is only 126. Given the relative qualities of Soviet champagne and Soviet
beer I would say that the planners have shown good judgment.

— January 6, 1950 (Letter 9) —

[Watkins here reports a visit to Moscow by Mao Tse-tung, whose Communist Chinese
government had been proclaimed on Sept. 30, 1949 but was not recognized by the
Western powers. Only in 1970 did Ottawa officially acknowledge communist rule in
China.]

I have the honour to confess that I found the Vishinsky reception to
which the Diplomatic Corps was invited on Stalin's seventieth birthday,
December 21st ... almost too dull for comment. Such as it was, however,
I should perhaps describe it briefly for the record. It may not be Stalin's
last decennial, since Georgians are notoriously long-lived, but whoever
is here for the next one might wish to make comparisons....

The pièce de résistance of the Bolshoi feast was, of course, General
Mao Tse-tung. His mere presence must have been more gratifying and
flattering than the most fulsome tributes. To have produced him for
the birthday was a genuine thaumaturgical triumph, whether Molotov's

or not we do not know. Everybody had guessed that something really spectacular was planned for December 21st, but Mao's arrival on December 16th seems to have come as a complete surprise to all the Western diplomats in Moscow, except the Icelandic Chargé (his wife is psychic) who had prophesied the evening before the exact moment of his arrival but had not thought it prudent to go to the station. It might have been expected that the Russians would keep Mao entirely to themselves, and in spite of their obvious desire to exploit the propaganda value of his presence, the foreign correspondents in Moscow were not invited to the Bolshoi, nor has any of them to the best of my knowledge set eyes on him in all the time that he has been here....

...I am inclined to agree with several experienced observers here who were of the opinion that the longer the Western Powers, and especially the United States, postponed recognition, the better pleased the Soviet Government would be. It has still, I think, a healthy respect for the wiliness and slipperiness of the Chinese and does not feel as sure of Mao Tse-tung as it could wish. His speech on arrival was cordial but there was no trace in it of the obsequiousness to which we have become accustomed in the speeches of prominent guests from Eastern Europe....

The Soviet desire to increase its prestige and influence is plain. The press keeps referring to the prompt recognition accorded to the new Government by the Soviet Union and emphasizing the aid given, and as of today's Pravda still being given, by the United States to Nationalist China, the pressure from the Congress and from the military to help Chiang Kai-Shek retain Formosa, and the wide-spread opposition to recognition and "the establishment of normal diplomatic relations with the Chinese People's Republic" ... One of the great virtues in American eyes of a certain small monarchy in the North of Europe is the alacrity with which it recognized the infant republic of the United States, and this not very important historical event still does yeoman service at all goodwill gatherings in much the same way that the Soviet Union's early recognition of the new China contributes to the atmosphere of brotherly love so thick in Moscow at the moment.... There can be little doubt, I think, that the victory of the Chinese Communists is felt both by the Party and the people as the most reassuring international phenomenon since the defeat of Hitler, and with a little more imagination we might all have guessed what Stalin's birthday surprise would be....

— **February 22, 1951 (Despatch 92)** —

[Watkins' description of casting a vote in the Soviet Union in the early 1950s would be little changed today.]

... In the school building directly across the street from the Embassy, there were two polling places on election day, the entrances to both decorated with the usual quantities of red bunting, patriotic slogans, and portraits of Stalin. At four o'clock on Sunday afternoon, Mr. Stansfield and I went into the more imposing of the two polling places to see if we could see a Soviet election in operation.

We followed a string of posters and bright red arrows to the second floor of the building, where we entered a large room. At one side, near the door, there was a row of tables, each presided over by a female official. I approached the nearest young lady and told her we wanted to see how people voted in the Soviet Union. She waved me towards a small man who was hovering in the background and who now approached us. I repeated to him that we were foreigners — Canadians — and that we wanted to see how people voted. He looked puzzled for a moment and then shook us both warmly by the hand and launched into an exposition of the Soviet election system without asking any questions about who we were or what we represented.

When voters came in, he said, they went first to the tables by which we were standing. Each table has a sign over it giving three or four letters of the alphabet, and voters went to the table corresponding to the initial letters of their surnames. On each table there was a partial voters list, one of which he showed us. It was a neat ledger made up of typewritten pages, each containing perhaps twenty to twenty-five names. There were approximately three thousand voters, he told us, in his polling district (he told us its boundaries by streets), and all their names were recorded in alphabetical order. Each voter was identified by a number, family name, and full first name and patronymic [based on the father's first name], year of birth, street, street number, and apartment number. Opposite this information, there was a space in each case for the initials of the scrutineer, to be entered when the voter collected his ballot. The page we saw had initials opposite all but one or two names.

After collecting his ballot, the voter could go directly to a battery of locked ballot boxes which stood at the other end of the room amid a tasteful arrangement of ferns and red bunting under a large colored picture of The Great Leader and Teacher [i.e., Stalin]. The voter could, if he wished, however, go instead into a small room past the ballot boxes and off to one side. We were duly escorted there and found that it contained three curtained booths. The ones we saw were prominently marked "4," "5," and "6," so I assume there must have been three others somewhere else although I did not see them. Our friend was at great pains to show us how tightly the curtains fitted over the booths and how completely private and secret they were. No one else could come in while the voter was there, he said, neither he himself nor any of his officials. Each booth, as he showed us, was provided with a table and a comfortable chair, and with pencils.

What, he asked rhetorically, would the voters write on their ballots? Many people (he answered himself) wished to write on their ballots "Long life and happiness to Comrade Joseph Vissarionovich Stalin!", "I am voting for peace!", or some other appropriate sentiment. Or again, it might be that a voter did not like the candidate and wished to strike out his name. In that case, he could do so. He might wish to add a few words explaining his objection to the candidate, perhaps he might feel that someone else would be a better deputy. In that case, he could write in another name. It was all, he emphasized again, absolutely free and absolutely secret. From the voting booths (if he had used them), the voter went back to the boxes and deposited his ballot.

The poll, we were told, opened at six o'clock in the morning and closed at midnight. The papers always report, after an election, that the majority of the voters had cast their ballots by an early hour in the day. Our observation confirmed that this was true; no voter came during the fifteen or twenty minutes we were there.

At midnight, our guide continued, the doors were locked, the ballot boxes opened, and the votes tabulated. All ballots on which the candidate's name had been crossed out and/or another name added were put to one side. The official remarked, in passing, that it was regarded as an unusually high percentage if three or four ballots had to be so segregated. Due attention was paid, also, to ballots which had anything else written upon them.

Watkins sent this despatch from the Canadian Embassy in Copenhagen as he made his way back to Canada on sick leave. It summarizes his impressions of Soviet life after about 29 months in Moscow. We have included the entire document as it effectively sets the scene of the late Stalin era, against which the thaw following Stalin's death may be measured. Watkins' comments about the refurbishing of the Soviet capital are perhaps over-

stated, as other Western diplomats in the period report that
Moscow remained run-down, with the exception of giant slab-
like apartment towers that found few admirers. To be noted are
Watkins' comments about China, where he departs from his usual
descriptive approach and recommends policy. Marginal notes on
the original document suggest a wide readership in Ottawa.

— March 29, 1951 (Despatch) —

On leaving Moscow after approximately two and a half years in the
Soviet Union, it might be useful to record a few final impressions.
What truth there is in the observation that to write about any country
one should have been there either ten days or ten years, however, is
peculiarly applicable to a country so vast and varied, so full of incon-
sistencies and contradictions, as the Soviet Union. A two-year term
spent mainly in the isolated society of the Moscow diplomatic corps
is barely enough to scratch the surface. The impressions so acquired
are inevitably superficial and often, no doubt, misleading. The Kremlin
divulges none of its secrets to the diplomatic corps. Attempts to divine
them are less confident in Moscow than in the Western press. A few
of the foreign specialists on Soviet affairs in Moscow develop a kind
of sixth sense which enables them to extract a good deal from the
atmosphere but experience has taught them to be undogmatic in their
interpretations and cautious in their predictions. One of their most
useful functions is to discourage facile speculation. In this despatch I
shall merely note some of the changes I have observed since arriving
in the Soviet Union in September, 1948, and record a few more general
impressions derived mainly from conversations with Soviet citizens in
several widely separated regions of the country. All the more experienced foreign observers in Moscow warned me on my arrival of the
futility of comparing conditions in the Soviet Union with conditions
in the West. The only valid standard of comparison was with conditions
as they had been in Russia itself before and after the Revolution, and
during the last World War. Russian soldiers who had served in Germany
and other central European countries had been able to compare their
own living conditions with those abroad and had been so critical on
their return that it had been necessary to put on a propaganda campaign
to "correct" the opinions they were disseminating, but the great masses
of the people knew almost nothing of life in the West and their only
standard of comparison was with what they had experienced in their
own country. Hence the actual level on which they were living was

much less important than the direction of the curve.

During the war the Soviet standard of living had declined sharply from the level it had reached in the Thirties. This was to be expected and was accepted as part of the cost of the war. The changeover from war-time to peace-time production, however, seems to have been more complicated and to have proceeded more slowly than had been antic-ipated with the result that in 1947 there was a serious production crisis and widespread discontent. By the middle of 1948 this critical point had been passed and the trend was again upwards. This upward trend has gradually gained momentum and the increase in the amount and variety of consumer goods available in the shops during the last eight-een months has been almost incredible. To the foreign observer it has been most noticeable in the appearance of the people. Two years ago they were all so badly dressed that foreigners were conspicuous wher-ever they went, merely by their clothes. Now they attract no particular attention even at the theatres, and the task of the militia men guarding foreign embassies has become increasingly difficult: they can no longer distinguish their own citizens by their clothes and are frequently embar-rassed to find that they have asked non-Russians about to enter a foreign embassy if they are not perhaps "making a mistake." The rapid increase in production is also apparent in the large number of new shops of all kinds and new restaurants that have opened, in the fleets of new taxis and cars, etc. When it is remembered that heavy industry is always given priority, this increase is still more impressive. It has been easily the most striking phenomenon of the last two years in the Soviet Union.

Food rationing had been dropped some time before I arrived, but there were still long queues for all sorts of supplies. Now there are seasonal shortages — the new lemon crop had just come in when I left, but the hens were staging their annual spring strike — but flour is the only important item of food that is restricted. It is sold only twice a year before festivals which call for a high consumption of griddle-cakes. Nobody supposes that flour is scarce, and the only prob-able explanation is that the State does not want people to bake their own bread or eat too many blinis [traditional Russian pancakes]. Together with the increase in the supply of consumer goods, there have been three substantial price reductions in the last two years. Food, clothing, shoes, and all sorts of everyday commodities are still fantast-ically high if the price is translated into dollars at the official rate of the rouble. Many of the prices seem high also in terms of the Soviet wage averages as we know them, but it has been very obvious recently that the great majority of the people have money to spend and are spending it. In the lower income groups the explanation seems to be that rents are almost negligible, that all the adult members of the family are gainfully employed, and that there are various supplements to the basic pay, of which we know very little. I was surprised to discover, for instance, that a schoolteacher is paid extra for every paper she marks, that a hotel maid gets a month's holiday at Sochi on the Black Sea with all expenses paid, etc. People in the higher income brackets are buying jewellery and other luxury items, possibly as an investment. There are many big signs admonishing citizens to save their money and put it in the bank, but it is likely that most of the people who got one rouble for ten when the currency changed in 1947 prefer to spend it.

The appearance of the city of Moscow itself has also improved greatly in the last two years. The street on which our Embassy stands, for instance, has changed almost beyond recognition. The cobblestones have been replaced by asphalt and all the old, tumbledown houses on both sides of the street have been remonted [refurbished] so that they look almost like new buildings. The same is true of many other streets in different parts of the city. There are still many very shabby sections, of course, but no doubt they will all be tackled in turn according to plan. In spite of a great deal of new building, some of it apparently very good and some incredibly bad, the housing situation in Moscow is still unsatisfactory even by Russian standards. The Government is now taking steps to reduce the metropolitan population and it has become very difficult for people living in the provinces to get permission to come to Moscow. Apartment space is allocated on a rigidly graded scale — at least in theory. A university professor, for instance, is entitled by law to two rooms of specified dimensions. If his wife is also doing scientific work, she is entitled to two additional rooms. The combination is a hypothetical four-room apartment plus kitchen, bath, etc. The only problem that remains is the purely physical one of finding the space. At present it is usually insoluble. At this point private enterprise may rear its ugly head and the professor may succeed in subletting an apartment at six or seven hundred roubles a month instead of the one hundred which the original lessee is paying to the State. It is safe to say that even those people who were fortunate enough to have had a four or five room apartment before the war are now living in unhygienically crowded conditions, for they all seem to be surrounded by a host of poor relations. Lower down in the scale the crowding is still worse, of course, and the resulting congestion is one of the militiamen's most difficult problems, since they are apparently expected to reduce it. "As soon as a family gets a proper apartment," one of them complained, "their relations swarm in like bedbugs and what can we do about it?" It would be a mistake to suppose, however, that this overcrowding is anything like the hardship to a Russian family (or to an Italian or an Icelandic family, for that matter) that it would be to a Canadian. In many cases it is a matter of choice. What the average Russian could not bear to contemplate would be the horror of having to live alone.

As long as the standard of living continues to improve, however gradually, there is not likely to be acute discontent with the regime. The Russian people are satisfied with so little that it is hard for us to imagine it. On the political side their demands are still more modest. They have never known political freedom as we understand it, and except for a few intellectuals they have no idea what it means. Their elections and their Supreme Soviet, which to us seem merely an elaborate farce, they take very seriously. Somehow or other the Government has managed to persuade the average citizen that his vote is extremely important. From talking to ordinary people in different parts of the country I feel sure that it is this conviction, more than the pressure from Party officials, which accounts for the large vote even in the far northern regions where it is not easy to get to the polling stations. The fact that they have no choice of parties or even of candidates does not seem in the least strange to them. It is sufficient to know that if they think a certain candidate has not taken his duties seriously enough, they can stroke out his name on the ballot. More intelligent or better informed people can understand that the single-party system strikes westerners as odd and undemocratic, but seem content with the explanation that the Communist Party is doing everything that could be done, or that it is surely more efficient to have a single party than the confusing multiplicity of parties one finds in a country like France, for instance. Some foreign writers have explained that the present system in the Soviet Union is educational and that as people become more experienced in the exercise of the franchise they will be given more choice. There may be some truth in this, but I can see nothing at present to indicate that the Communist Party plans to share its authority with any other.

In spite of the lack of opposition parties, however, the Politburo cannot entirely disregard public opinion. There are other ways in which it can make itself felt than in elections. One of them is in declining production, and to this the Politburo is extremely sensitive. Hence the constant propaganda to explain to the masses that what is being done is in their best interests. This is cleverly done and is generally success-ful. The ordinary citizen seems genuinely convinced that he has a share in all the great State enterprises, and the recent announcement of the vast new irrigation and power projects has obviously fired the popular imagination, as it was intended to do, in all parts of the country. In the case of the collectivization of agriculture in the Ukraine in the Thirties, however, the Government did not succeed, as Stalin explained to Churchill, in convincing the farmers that it would ultimately be to their advantage. Those who could not be convinced were starved out or transported to Siberia. But such ruthless methods are dangerous to the regime, and if it had not been for the threat from Germany, it is probable that a more gradual transformation would have been preferred. In Great Russia the Bolsheviks were frequently forced to come to terms with recalcitrant groups and they prefer to avoid a showdown if they can. However badly they may gauge Western psychology in their prop-aganda efforts, it is generally admitted that they understand the psychol-ogy of their own people, including the non-Russian races, extremely well. A tremendous effort is constantly being made, by both positive and negative means, to mould public opinion. The intensity of the effort illustrates at once the importance of the task and the difficulty of it.

The isolation of the Russian people is about as complete as the Kremlin intends it to be. Soviet citizens can apparently travel to any place they wish within the boundaries of the Soviet Union and they are still nomadic enough to take as full advantage of this as their means permit. Indeed, many seem to travel without much means and for no good reason. They would be no less eager to travel abroad but only very few can get exit visas even for the neighbouring satellite countries. The ban on travel abroad, however, is probably much less felt in such an enormous country with such a great variety of climates, landscapes, languages, and cultures than it would be in most European countries. It is about as difficult for foreigners to obtain entry visas to the Soviet Union as for Soviet citizens to obtain exit visas. A good many cultural or peace delegations come for brief visits, but their programmes are always carefully planned and their contacts with the natives must be relatively few. The Soviet press is, of course, completely controlled and prints only what the people want to read. Occasionally they repro-duce speeches, articles, or diplomatic notes from abroad which come as a surprise to foreigners in Moscow and can hardly be less of a surprise to Soviet readers. It is not easy to guess the reasons for these exceptions to the general rule. For the most part, however, the Soviet press is extremely dull. It gives a ridiculously distorted picture of the West, and it was refreshing to find that a good deal of this nonsense is received with healthy skepticism. Its half-truths are more frequent and insidious than its untruths, and unfortunately the Western press, and especially the American, provides excellent material for the Soviet propaganda machine. Quotations from senators and congressmen are popular and the most outrageous ones are almost invariably exact translations. Foreign radio programmes are so effectively jammed that they cannot be heard at all in Moscow and only with great difficulty in other parts of the country.

All observers in Moscow agree that the Soviet people in all parts of the country in which we have had any contact with them want peace. They suffered horribly in the last war and in the devastated regions particularly are still suffering from its effects. Their losses were enormous and almost everybody one meets has lost one or more close relatives. In a defensive war they would undoubtedly fight and fight well, but unlike the Germans they are not a bellicose people. As [British historian Arnold] Toynbee points out, they have been more aggressed against than aggressing in their history, and many of them have experienced two German invasions and the war of [Allied] intervention [at the close of the First World War]. If their rulers wanted war, of course, all the vast propaganda machine would be brought into operation to convince them that their country was not the aggressor and that their cause was just, but they are not stupid or uncritical and the Government would have to choose its ground very carefully. A threat from Germany would rally them more quickly around their Government than a threat from any other quarter.

Most observers here agree that the Soviet Government does not want to risk war at the present time. Whatever they can get by other methods or by local wars in which they need not become involved, they will, of course, take. They know quite well that they could occupy Western Europe in a comparatively short time but they also know that this would inevitably bring them into conflict with the United States and that their productive capacity is and will remain for a long time much below that of the United States. They know, too, that the industrial progress they have made and the great industrial projects they have planned would be set back for years if they were involved in a World War, and the people as a whole know this just as well as the Kremlin does. It has been argued that if they have decided that war is inevitable it would be much more to their advantage to have it now than later, when Western Europe has built up its defenses. This seems logical, but there are no indications at present that they would be willing to take the risk. As far as can be seen in the parts of the country open to us, it appears that just now they have reached a low point, for them, in the number of men they have under arms. They seem to have released a large proportion of their older classes without calling in an equivalent number — perhaps because of the demands on manpower made by the new industrial projects announced last year. It is probable that the deficiency will soon be made up, but if they had expected to be involved in war very soon, it is unlikely that they would have released so many. It is also interesting to note that so far as we can discover no attempt is being made to provide bomb shelters in large cities like Moscow and Leningrad.

The peace campaign, as seemed probable from the beginning, is being pressed to the limit. Until recently the propaganda has been reassuring: the broad masses of the people everywhere are opposed to war and will not permit the instigators of war to plunge the world into misery again. Stalin's *Pravda* [the major Soviet daily] interview was less reassuring. Although he said that war was not inevitable, he was not so certain that the people might not be deceived and led into it by the instigators of war. The more intelligent part of the population seems to have taken this as a warning and the recent increase in the military budget must have confirmed it, nor could Stalin's statement that their present military forces were only about half those of their potential enemies have made them feel any more secure. In spite of this, however, the peace campaign continues at full blast in the press and, however insincere it may be, it is not the best preparation for a war mentality and would certainly have to be changed if war in the near future were contemplated. For this reason it is important to watch closely for changes in the propaganda line.

The feeling of confidence so obvious last year when the Chinese nationalists were defeated seems to have ebbed somewhat, partly, no doubt, as a result of the Korean war and partly, perhaps, because the Russians still do not feel very sure of China. From various small pointers observed by Western diplomats here, it seems clear that China is not regarded and does not regard itself as a satellite in the sense that Poland, Czechoslovakia, Hungary and the rest are satellites. The Russians are still being elaborately careful in how they handle the Chinese and must be secretly grateful for the circumstances which have prevented any closer relationships between the Chinese and the West. Whether they are really afraid of Mao Tse-tung turning out to be another Tito, I should not venture to guess, but at least they have not forgotten their great disappointment in Chiang Kai-Shek in 1927. It has been suggested, too, that the Russians are by no means averse to having the Chinese wear themselves down a little more in fighting the United Nations in Korea. If having convinced ourselves that Tito, although a Communist, is not such a bad fellow after all, it would not strain our principles too much to discover a few ingratiating traits in Mao Tse-tung (once the Korean business is settled, of course). It would, I believe, worry the Kremlin as much as anything else we could do. At a public lecture recently the speaker asked sarcastically what the West was offering the Asian countries, and answered it as follows: "The return of the feudal system and the bankers, and such discredited figures as Chiang Kai-Shek, Syngman Rhee and Bao Dai, but these offers do not tempt the nationalist populations of Asia." It costs the Russians nothing to play up nationalism in Asia just as energetically as they crush it in Eastern Europe, but perhaps this game could be made less easy for them.

Social conditions in the Far East facilitate the Soviet propaganda effort and so, I fear, do social conditions in the Middle East. It may be that as the Communist parties in Western Europe continue to lose ground, the Soviet Union will decide to concentrate more on Asia. It is clear that unless it becomes involved in war the Soviet Union will make vast progress in industrialization in the next few years. Looked at from Asia the progress of the Soviet Union in the last thirty years is already sufficiently impressive, and if it continues at the present speed it is bound to influence Asian opinion more and more, unless the West can assist the Asian countries to meet their difficult problems more rapidly and effectively than it has been able to do so far.

Ambassador, Settling in,
Spring and Summer, 1954

— March 25, 1954 (Letter 206) —

[The following was written a bare three weeks after Watkins arrived in the Soviet capital as ambassador. Based on first impressions, the letter nevertheless affirms a new post-Stalin willingness by the Kremlin to place relations on a more congenial footing.]

On Monday afternoon, March 22, I was given appointments to call on the three Deputy Foreign Ministers, Messrs. [Andrei] Gromyko, [Valerian] Zorin and [Vasily] Kuznetzov.[1] Translators were present at all three interviews but most of the conversation was direct in either Russian or English.

Mr. Gromyko looked slightly less sour than the last time I saw him ... and seemed to be making an effort to appear friendly, although without conspicuous success. He said that he had heard that I had spoken Russian to [Soviet President] Mr. [Kliment E.] Voroshilov so I replied in Russian and after a time he admitted that he spoke a little English. It soon became apparent that he could understand anything I said quite easily without any help from the interpeter and he often answered in English before the interpreter could begin to translate. (The British Ambassador [Sir William Hayter] has since mentioned that he always goes alone to see Gromyko and they discuss all their business in English.)

The conversation was mainly about changes in Moscow since I was last here, the new buildings and the new Metro stations, of which I had made a tour the day before, and the theatre. When I said that I supposed he was too busy to go much to the theatre, he replied with a smile: "Oh, we have a very strict regime here now, you know. We have to work from nine to six." He wanted to know what hours we worked in Ottawa and was obviously impressed to learn that we no longer worked on Saturdays. (The Austrian Minister says that the new schedule is the greatest sacrifice that Russian office workers have been asked to make; a purge is nothing by comparison, for it affects only the purgees, so to speak, but this Draconian regulation has revolutionized the time-honoured habits of the whole civil service and upset their family life and their whole pattern of living.) When I was about to leave, Mr. Gromyko said that he hoped I would enjoy my stay in Moscow and that he would always be available if there was anything I wished to discuss with him or if he could be of any help to me. He has lost a good deal of weight since I last saw him and looked rather tired. (The American Ambassador [Charles Bohlen] asked whether I had noticed that his rapid loss of weight was unnatural and probably due to cancer.)....

The general impression gained from the three interviews was that the Russian officials are anxious to behave in a more civilized and normal way than heretofore. This is also the impression they make when they come with their wives to diplomatic receptions. There is definitely a "new look" and if it is not discouraged it may gradually become more natural. Aside from temperament, which is of course important, it is probably most difficult for those who have had most practice in the old style. The Netherlands Ambassador says that if you begin an interview with Gromyko with a little light conversation he warms up and is easier to talk to on business matters.

Watkins reported on numerous occasions his conversations with the Kazakeviches, husband and wife academics with whom he had socialized during his stint as chargé d'affaires. Here he reintroduces them to the Department of External Affairs, and describes the first two of what were to be many meetings.

The son of White Russians, Vladimir was raised in St. Petersburg (Leningrad), but the family moved east when his father became a manager for the Chinese Eastern railway. Vladimir arrived in the United States as a displaced person in the late 1920s, without a Soviet or American passport and without any revolutionary convictions. He fell in with a Communist group on the West Coast, and although he never joined the Communist party, Vladimir's overriding ambition was to return to the U.S.S.R. to become a Soviet citizen. To this end, he would deliver odd bits of intelligence to the Soviet consulate in New York in the hope he would be rewarded with settlement in the Soviet Union. Watkins met Vladimir at Columbia University in 1930 and apparently kept up contact throughout the 1930s and early 1940s. In 1943, Vladimir landed a U.S. Army teaching job at Cornell University's Russian Institute, and for a short time delivered high quality intelligence to the New York consulate until a newspaperman exposed him as a Communist sympathizer. He was described by fellow spy Elizabeth Bentley as "a tall, hungry-looking Russian with glasses and a perpetually absent-minded air." Bentley's confession before a committee of the U.S. Congress in 1949 prompted the Soviet government to bring Vladimir and his wife to Moscow where they both secured teaching posts. Bentley's Out of Bondage, *published in 1951, exposed Kazakevich publicly as a spy and should have been known to*

Watkins, if not to External Affairs. (Unfortunately, a series of letters about the Kazakeviches that Watkins sent to Ottawa in the spring of 1951 has not been located.)

The Kazakeviches' Moscow apartment was doubtless riddled with hidden microphones, and, as Watkins notes, they managed to obtain a telephone shortly before his arrival in Moscow. They were almost certainly a useful conduit for whatever intelligence could be obtained from the new Canadian ambassador, and Watkins in turn did not hesitate to pump them for information. All this was unspoken between them, and the despatches do suggest a genuine friendship and mutual affection for things cultural.

Watkins' acceptance into the homes of Soviet citizens was in marked contrast to the experience of the American ambassador to Moscow. Charles Bohlen and his wife were never invited to a private home in the Soviet Union during all their years there, even in the post-Stalin thaw. The British ambassador, Sir William Hayter, recalls that in contrast to the enforced isolation of the Stalin period, from 1953 on he and his wife got to know "hundreds, perhaps thousands of Soviet citizens," but none of them well. Watkins, on the other hand, cultivated a circle of Soviet friends whom he came to know intimately.

— May 6, 1954 (Letter 284) —

The day after my arrival in Moscow was announced in *Pravda* I received a telephone call from Mr. Vladimir D. Kazakevich to welcome me back on behalf of his wife, Emily Grace Kazakevich, and himself. He invited me to lunch at the Grand Hotel on Sunday, March 7, and then took me to see their new apartment....

(You may remember that I saw the Kazakeviches several times in the spring of 1951 and reported at some length on my conversations with them. I had met him first at International House in New York in the fall of 1930. He had recently taken his Master's degree in economics at Columbia University, where he had specialized in business cycles under Mitchell, Willis and others, and was employed in some kind of statistical research bureau headed by a Russian economist named Kuznetzov, I think. Later he taught economics at Columbia and at the Bankers' Institute. His parents were White Russians, members of the old Leningrad aristocracy. His father, who had been Assistant General Manager of the Chinese Eastern Railway, remained in Harbin [in

Manchuria] after the Russian Revolution and died there some years ago; the mother is still living in China. I had not seen Kazakevich for a number of years when he turned up as a lecturer on economics at the Russian Institute which was started at Cornell when I was working there on Old Norse in 1943. In the meantime he had divorced his pretty but rather crazy Jewish wife and married Emily Grace, an American girl of a well-to-do family, who had spent much of her childhood in Muskoka [in south central Ontario], where her uncle, the late Dr. Parfitt, had established one of the best known private T.B. sanitoria on the continent, the Calidor. Mrs. Kazakevich has a Ph.D. from Yale in Ancient History. When New York began to get too hot for people of as radical views as the Kazakeviches, they left in circumstances which I described in some detail in letters from Moscow....)

Kazakevich was waiting for me at the entrance of the Metropole Hotel as arranged in our telephone conversation. He looked just about the same, except perhaps a little thinner and greyer. He was wearing a rough, shabby-looking brown tweed overcoat with a ratty brown fur collar and hat. When we were sitting at the table, I noticed that the cuffs of his white shirt were badly frayed and that his dark grey suit would not last much longer. It was probably a cheap one to start with, for he never cared at all about clothes and spent all his money on books, and he does not seem to have bought anything here.

They had lived in hotels for two years after I left in 1951, he told me, but now had a fairly good apartment in one of the new buildings on the outskirts of the city.... It was very comfortable, and Emily, who is a complete blue-stocking and loathes housework, would have been happy, I think, to have lived there indefinitely, if the management had not kept moving them from one apartment to another. For a while they had a very grand one on the top floor overlooking the Red Square, but they had had to give it up to deputies of the Supreme Soviet and were allotted a much less attractive one. In all they were moved about ten times in two years.

Finally they got permission to occupy their present quarters a few months ago. The building was still far from finished and there was scaffolding all over the place when they moved in. It was warm enough, even too warm, but the central hot-water station was not yet functioning and they had to heat water on the gas stove. The Soviet builders were learning as they went along, Kazakevich said. The central station to supply hot water to all the apartments in the dozen or more which formed the complex to which theirs belonged was a big advance. Unfortunately for them, however, the idea of built-in closet space had occurred

to the architects only after this complex was planned. All the large
new buildings on the other side of the street had built-in closet space,
he noted with envy. And no wonder; for the Kazakeviches do not
possess any of the huge wardrobes with which the average Russian
family is equipped and seemed to have most of their clothing hanging
on hooks on the bathroom door....

I remarked that if this suburb was typical of other parts of the outskirts
there must be much less crowding than when I was here three years
ago. Kazakevich said that there were many similar developments but
that the congestion was not much relieved. In the first place, the overcrowding when so many people had moved in during the war years
had been quite fantastic. In the second, in spite of efforts to discourage
people from moving into Moscow, the population was still increasing
rapidly. The construction programme itself added to the problem it was
planned to solve. Thousands of labourers were brought in from the
villages to work on the new buildings. They lived in dormitories and
left their families in the country. But with their relatively high wages
they were able to buy nylons and hats for their wives, who rapidly
developed a taste for these and other urban amenities, and insisted on
moving to the city. The men then demanded apartments similar to the
ones they were building, and it did not look as if the supply would
ever catch up with the demand.

As we walked along the wide, well-paved Novo-Peschanaya Street,
Kazakevich pointed to various shop fronts on the ground floor of the
large apartment houses. There was the main grocery shop where they
bought provisions. Across the street a new restaurant was to open in
a few weeks. Beside it was a window advertising that a new cleaning
and pressing establishment was starting up. These neighbourhood shops
would soon make it unnecessary for suburban dwellers to go into the
centre for any of their ordinary every-day needs....

The entrance to the Kazakevich's apartment house was off a large paved
courtyard almost completely surrounded by large blocks of apartments.
Several Pobedas were standing in the yard, evidently the private cars
of the more affluent inhabitants, and many small children were playing
there. At one end was the low building for the hot-water supply, of
which Kazakevich was so proud. He pointed out that the ground floor
of their house was occupied by the local office of the M.V.D. [secret
police], and said that this gave them additional protection and effec-

tively discouraged hooligans. The entrance was as drab and dirty as most Moscow entrances and the lift was the standard contraption. Fortunately it was working and the old attendant, although drunk enough to be garrulous, was on duty, for the Kazakevich's apartment is on the sixth floor. I imagine that it is the size to which they are legally entitled because they had two good-sized living rooms. If a Soviet wife is also an intellectual worker, she is entitled to working space equivalent to her husband's. Kazakevich had made bookcases for his books in his own room and for his wife's in hers out of packing-boxes. They were practical, if not elegant, and I congratulated Kazakevich, who I do not suppose had ever had a hammer in his hand before. Except for desks, tables, a divan and a few chairs, they had very little furniture. Since they had no place to store their trunks, they had set them around on the floor and covered them with oriental rugs from Mrs. Kazakevich's mother's apartment in New York so that they could be used to sit on if they had more guests than chairs. Kazakevich's room, in which we had tea, had windows on two sides and was light and airy. The wall-paper was in Soviet taste — a large and striking conventionalized flower pattern in pale grey on a bright blue background. The wallpaper in the other rooms was still gaudier and Mrs. Kazakevich was planning to redecorate at the first opportunity. A leak in the bathroom ceiling had finally been repaired before the plaster fell down but a section of the impressive white tiling in the bathroom had fallen out between the day of my visit and the next time I saw them. The plumbing was a great improvement on anything I had seen here before; there was even a built-in bathtub. They had been promised a telephone for months and the wiring had been finished for weeks, but they only got it installed about a week ago....

I did not think that Mrs. Kazakevich looked very happy and she is obviously rather lonely and homesick. They still get letters from relations and friends in the United States but not so many as when I saw them three years ago. Kazakevich remarked that if it were not for his work at the Institute he would prefer to live in Leningrad, but of course like all natives of St. Petersburg he is a strong local patriot. It was a much more beautiful city, he said, and not so overgrown and hectic as Moscow. There was not much left here of the old historic Moscow except the Kremlin and he did not much care for the kind of Russian Chicago that was replacing it. The new tall buildings looked too much like Florentine wedding cakes for his taste, and the shoddiness of much of the new building and the lack of proper maintenance was depressing. However, he did not know how he could have kept out of jail in the

United States under McCarthyism and it would probably have been more difficult to start over again in London or Paris than it had been here.

Kazakevich is now employed in the Institute of Economics, his wife in the Institute of Ancient History, which has offices in the same building and not very far from our Embassy. It takes 40 minutes by bus and metro from his apartment to the office, and under the new regulations he has to sign in every morning at nine and sign out every evening at six. He has never been used to keeping such regular office hours and finds it a bore. Nobody seems to care where you are between those two fixed times, he says, and he is often out of the office for several hours at a time. In fact he said that he would like to visit the Tretyakovsky Gallery with me some day during office hours and that it would be quite in order for him to do so. He spends most of every morning reading the papers and especially the foreign press, British, French, American, Swiss, etc. He referred in particular to the *London Times, Le Monde,* the *New York Times* and *Herald-Tribune,* the *Neue Zuricher Zeiting,* the *Economist* and various monthly or quarterly journals of economics. They have a large economics library in the Institute and buy many foreign works but he complained that they were sometimes slow in getting things he had ordered. Sometimes they have quite a search for odd bits of information suddenly requested from exalted heights. Not long ago Mr. [Lazar] Kaganovich [member of the party Praesidium] asked how many bicycles there were in Japan, and the answer had finally been found in a British magazine devoted to Japanese affairs. Again he had asked for the number of television sets in Japan and by chance it was discovered in some foreign newspaper that the Japanese were only now planning to make a start in the television field. These examples were given to me merely to illustrate some of the tasks for which Kazakevich, as head of a section, was responsible, and I did not venture to ask the reason for Mr. Kaganovich's preoccupation with Japan....

Mrs. Kazakevich does not have to keep regular office hours and does most of her work at home. She goes to the office every other day or so, sometimes in the morning and sometimes in the afternoon. The atmosphere was much less hectic in the Ancient History Institute than in the Economics Institute — presumably because people like Mr. Kaganovich are not so urgently concerned about the details of daily life in Ancient Greece. Just now Mrs. Kazakevich was working against

a dead-line in editing a collection of studies on Greek archaeology but
normally she was under no pressure to produce things in a hurry. She
usually writes on her own subject in English and has it translated but
recently she has been doing some writing in Russian. She reads it easily
but says that her ability to speak has not improved very much as she
does not get much practice.

They both seem to spend practically all their time on their work and
to have very little social life. Nor do they go very often to the theatre,
whether because they do not feel they can afford it or because they
have not the energy, I do not know. They did not say what their salaries
were but I should guess that while they are a good deal less than that
of a full university professor (5,000 roubles a month) they are well
above the average. The fact that Mrs. Kazakevich cannot cook — she
speaks of always opening a can of beans when they haven't time to
go out for a meal and they both look as if they could do with better
food — must make life a good deal more expensive than it would be
otherwise.

Kazakevich said that the main difference between Russian life now
and as he remembered it from the old days in Leningrad was the present
lack of social life. The Russians had always been very hospitable and
fond of company and were always dropping in on each other for the
evening or having friends in for meals. The main reason for the change,
he said, was lack of space. Many of their colleagues still had only one
room and used a communal kitchen. This made entertaining practically
impossible. Others had dachas outside the city and spent anywhere
from one hour to two in transit. This meant leaving the office at six
and not getting home until eight or after. It also meant starting out in
the morning around seven, and even if they could persuade their friends
to make the long trip out and in to visit them, they would not have
the energy to do it very often....

[Two weeks later, Watkins invited the Kazakeviches out for lunch.]

Regarding the change in atmosphere since Stalin's death, the Kazakeviches thought that while distinctly perceptible it had been and would
continue to be very gradual and would depend on how successfully
efforts to effect a relaxation of tension in international relations generally could be pursued. In this sphere they regarded United States policy
as the most unpredictable element and thought that the Americans were
capable at any moment of making some rash move which would inevitably precipitate a world war, although it seemed to them that it should

be plain to everyone that neither China nor the Soviet Union had any desire to be involved....

Watkins' description of celebrations commemorating the union of The Ukraine with Russia illustrates the barren ground diplomats had to till in analyzing power games in the Kremlin. Such seeming trivialities as the color of Malenkov's suit, the expression on the face of Khrushchev in official photographs, the arrangement of seats on a podium — all were carefully winnowed for clues. It should be recalled that not since the interregnum of 1924 - 1927, between the death of Lenin and the ascendancy of Stalin, were such mundane details regarded as quite so vital.

— June 1, 1954 (Despatch 342) —

For more than a month now Moscow has been celebrating in various ways the tercentenary of the union of the Ukraine with Russia by the Treaty of Pereyaslav in 1654. The press has carried innumerable articles extolling the virtues and achievements of the now brotherly, now sisterly, but rarely sexless Ukrainian S.S.R. and its invaluable collaboration in the building of communism. History has been revamped to serve the occasion. Unconditional submission to an autocratic Moscow Czar was a piece of far-sighted statesmanship which was to lead eventually to the present glorious independence of the Ukrainian Republic....

[The celebrations included a special session of the Supreme Soviet on May 29 attended by Mikoyan, Bulganin, Khrushchev, Malenkov, and other Soviet leaders.]

The sensation of the day ... was Mr. Malenkov's new suit. We were too far away from it to appreciate the fine points but at least it was very light in colour — in fact almost cream- coloured. With it he wore a white shirt — not even the sharp eyes of the newspapermen could discern whether it had a stripe in it or not — and a tie. His long black oily-looking hair was neatly parted. He smiled broadly and frequently seemed to be joking with Bulganin, Khrushchev, and the babushka [unidentified "granny" who also occupied a front row seat] a good deal of the time instead of listening to the speeches, in which he must have been reasonably sure there would be no surprises. At appropriate moments he applauded, I should guess quite noiselessly, with his small plump tapered hands barely raised above the table — by contrast with

Mr. Khrushchev, who lifts his hands high enough to spoil the camera's view of his face and claps lustily. At climatic points, such as the announcements of the award of the Order of Lenin to the Republic of the Ukraine and to the City of Kiev, he stood up with the rest and clapped visibly if not audibly. For all his laughing, chatting, and fumbling in his pockets for papers, Mr. Malenkov seemed to be as solid and patient a sitter as anybody in the front row. Mr. Mikoyan was either figuring or doodling throughout....

Mr. Malenkov wore his new suit again at the concert [held that night at 8 PM]. It may well be the only one he has. None of us had ever seen him before (except on the ikons [i.e., party posters]) in anything but his dark party tunic looking both unkempt and glum, and the combination of the light suit, shirt, tie, haircomb and smile seemed to mark the beginning of a new era. It is probably correct to conclude that the Russian Revolution has now reached a point of respectability at which the party tunic can be abandoned to the Chinese in favour of an approximation of ordinary Western attire.

At the Bolshoi [ballet] Mr. Malenkov and his associates occupied the centre box in the first balcony directly opposite the stage. The fear of assassination, the United States ambassador remarked, seems to have diminished; Stalin, who had something of an obsession on the subject, usually preferred to sit in one of the front side boxes, which offer a less easy target. There seems, he said, to have been a general exodus from the Kremlin recently, and it is believed that Malenkov himself now lives in a modest old bourgeois mansion, but emphatically not a palace, near the Finnish Legation and not very far from us....

During the first half of the concert (there were fortunately no speeches) Marshal Bulganin, in uniform, sat in the centre of the box with Malenkov and Khrushchev on his right and Mikoyan and two others on his left. In the second half Malenkov sat in the centre with Khrushchev and Bulganin on his right. This was probably done deliberately out of a malicious and perverted sense of humour in order to tease and confuse the Western diplomats and correspondents whose solemn studies of the order of precedence at public gatherings, in the Party ikons (it was still Malenkov, Molotov, Khrushchev, Kaganovich, Mikoyan in the displays of the tercentenary) and in the press must be well known to Soviet officials....

In the procession up the steps to the top of the Lenin-Stalin mausoleum in the Red Square on Sunday morning, May 30, at precisely ten o'clock, it could be said, I think, that Mr. Malenkov was always at least half a step ahead of Mr. Khrushchev. Again he wore his cream-coloured suit, this time with a white, probably straw, hat. Mr. Khrushchev wore a light grey suit and what looked like an identical white hat. In the pictures published in the press the next day both hats were raised to approximately the same height and there was nothing to suggest ... that Mr. Khrushchev might be forging ahead of Mr. Malenkov.

— June 18, 1954 (Despatch 394) —

[More speculation on the rivalry between Malenkov and Khrushchev.]

For several weeks, the Italian Ambassador, Count di Stefano, with saccharine smiles and knowing looks, has been advising everybody to keep an eye on the calendar, for June is a month when strange and sudden things are apt to happen in the Kremlin. Nothing, so far as I know, has happened yet but certainly during recent weeks a number of members of the diplomatic corps have been suggesting that something is in the air and, increasingly, as the first anniversary of the Beria business approaches, every move of Messrs. Malenkov and Khrushchev is scrutinized intently. Every morning *Pravda* is opened by many in the pleasurable anticipation that Mr. Malenkov may have reasserted his pre-eminence; each time Mr. Khrushchev mounts a podium a faction of the corps expects that he has come to Beria Caesar and not to praise him.

Those of my colleagues who were caught napping last time are determined not to be again; on all sides premonitions are being patched up into predictions and I have no doubt that the diplomatic bags have lately carried a heavy load of ''ifs'' and ''buts'' and ''on the other hands.'' Certainly, as I have reported, there has been no lack of evidence during recent months to imply that the Party and Mr. Khrushchev are increasing their activity, and if the straws in the wind which have suggested this are small, they have been many....

The *New York Times* representative, Harrison Salisbury, at the time of the May 1st celebration, submitted to the censor (on the suggestion of the U.S. Ambassador) a story which speculated on possible rivalry between Messrs. Malenkov and Khrushchev. The censor cut a reference to Malenkov's pre-eminent position in the pictures of the members of the party Praesidium which formed part of the decorations. (Officially, still, the order was Malenkov, Molotov, Khrushchev). After 48 hours delay the story was passed.

This is interesting but not necessarily important; the censor's hesitancy might well have been on the grounds that the reference was in disagreement with the theory of collective government....

All that we can conclude with certainty is that, as before, the Party runs the country and although Stalin was the Party we are not sure now who runs it. I, myself, don't think that there is any indication that a crisis is approaching in a struggle for power in the Kremlin, not yet at any rate, although there do seem to be indications that in personalities, if not in policies, there lie the seeds of such a crisis. And these recent developments underline what we already knew, that Malenkov and Khrushchev are the two main forces to be considered. It should be kept in mind, however, that the old guard of Molotov, Kaganovich, Voroshilov and Mikoyan, probably still have the balance of power, and like the army are probably unwilling to permit personal feuding to endanger the security of the State. The British Ambassador, Sir William Hayter, thinks that if anything were wrong there would not be so many premonitory symptoms and he feels, perhaps rather more confidently than I do, that all of these are explainable on other grounds than that of rivalry between Malenkov and Khrushchev. The U.S. Ambassador, Mr. Bohlen, on the other hand, apparently thinks that although none of them are individually of much importance, the cumulative effect is considerable. He does not, however, think that it is likely that a final crisis in the leadership will occur before the harvest this year, or in 1955 shows how the government's agricultural policy is working; this will be the supreme test of Khrushchev. And he is not convinced that there will be such a crisis so soon. I agree, and I am inclined to think that although Khrushchev has now assumed an importance second only to Malenkov and may even in some respects be equal to him in the actual exercise of power, nevertheless this is an institutional rather than a personal matter and eventual conflict, if any, will be largely for institutional rather than personal reasons.

A Trip through
Soviet Central Asia

September to October, 1954

The following despatches record parts of a fifteen-day trip Watkins took to Soviet Central Asia from September 21 to October 6, 1954. He was among the first Western diplomats to pass through the region after travel restrictions began to be lifted in June 1953, during the post-Stalin thaw. (The British Ambassador Sir William Hayter also visited the area in 1954, and the American ambassador, Charles Bohlen, toured the Central Asian republics in the spring of 1955.) Watkins travelled alone, often wearing his "tibiteika" or Moslem skull cap, so that he was able to mingle unobtrusively with the native populations. Virtually everyone he met spoke Russian.

The area, forming the larger part of ancient Turkestan, is bordered on the east by China, on the south by Afghanistan and Iran, and by the Caspian Sea on the west. The region has a tortuous history. A vital trading crossroads for hundreds of years, Turkestan suffered numerous invasions, led by Alexander the Great, Ghenghis Khan and Tamerlane among others. The Moslem religion was introduced about the year 800 AD, and became dominant. Unreliable water supplies and pasturage encouraged nomadic cultures, and even into the twentieth century the area was home to wandering tribes. The days of the great caravans faded when in the early modern age Western Europe discovered ocean routes to the Orient. Turkestan was ruled by city states until about the 1880s, when China, Afghanistan and Russia brought sections under their central governments. A civil war broke out following the 1917 Russian Revolution and touched the region, and it was not until the early 1920s that Soviet rule was affirmed. Eventually the Russian-ruled areas of Central Asia were divided ethnically into the Uzbek, Tadjik, and Kirghis Soviet republics. Parts of Turkestan were also severed to form parts of the Kazakh and Turkmen Soviet republics. The cultural heritage of the region is largely Persian, although Turk migrations between the ninth and twelfth centuries made Turkic the dominant language. The new Soviet regime set about in the 1920s to undo centuries of illiteracy and economic backwardness in Central Asia, and to accommodate Moslem sensibilities within the atheist Marxist state. (Based on Watkins' reports, Islam appeared not to have been passed on to the post-revolution generation, although currently this trend appears to be reversing.)

Much of Soviet Central Asia sees little rainfall, so that efficient irrigation is essential to maintain the modern regional economies. As a farmer's son, Watkins could provide a quick assessment of Soviet successes and failures in this regard. The area was also being monitored by NATO for signs of military buildup. The Soviet Union, along with Britain, had invaded neighboring Persia (Iran) during the Second World War to topple a regime sympathic to the Axis. Although Stalin declared his intention to pull out within six months of the end of the war, the Kremlin attempted to incorporate Azerbaijan, the northern Iranian province, into the Soviet empire. The military pull-out was late, and Soviet agents helped establish a puppet regime in the north in 1946, although it was quashed in December by the Iranian army. Iran fell more and more into the Western fold, and there were fears the Soviets might launch a drive through to the Persian Gulf. The death of Stalin brought a policy turnabout, and by December 1954, outstanding conflicts between Iran and the U.S.S.R. were resolved. Even so, the border areas remained heavily militarized and were off limits to the West. Watkins was unable to report much that was useful to NATO analysts.

Watkins' real interest, in any case, was in exploring the relics of ancient empires and talking at length with the locals. These conversations — with students, poets, academics, cab drivers and librarians — often became spirited once Watkins revealed he was from the West, as such visitors were rare. Sometimes these chance meetings would take place in the local Park of Rest and Culture, where films and other amusements were available for a nominal fee. The parks, created by the Soviet government, drew great crowds in the summer and Watkins' frequent strolls through these centres were an adaptation to local conditions. An evening visit to a park in modern North America conjures up unsavory images, but in the Soviet Union it was an occasion for relaxation and entertainment in the company of neighbours and friends.

The RCMP interrogation revealed that Watkins had at least two homosexual liaisons in Central Asia. One was with a poet we identify as Nazir Akhimich Akhundi, whom Watkins describes in great detail in the despatch referring to the city of Tashkent (No. 47). Akhundi was a free-spirited, independent thinker, not an ideal candidate for co-opting into a secret police blackmail attempt. Watkins apparently confessed in 1964 that the affair was over as quickly as it began; the secret police either did not try to exploit the relationship, or they tried and failed.

The other such liaison, though, was seized upon by Soviet agents. As the RCMP learned years later, Watkins' had an affair during the trip with a young man, in his early twenties, named Kamahl, who apparently worked as a clerk on a farming co-operative. No such name appears in the despatches. However, Despatch 35 describes a young man who may be the elusive Kamahl. The despatch contains account of Watkins' visit to Stalinabad (now called Dushanbe), and refers to an 18-year-old Uzbek named Khalek Abdu. Khalek was enrolled in first-year economics at university and planned to study in Moscow for a diplomatic career. He was also keenly interested in Watkins. The two walked and talked for hours together in the streets of Stalinabad. Khalek gave his address to Watkins, who later sent him a postcard which was unanswered by January 1955. Khalek may have contacted Watkins again between February 1955 and March 1956, the likely period in which the secretly-photographed liaison in the Moscow hotel room occurred.

Details of the trip were reported by Watkins many months after his return to Moscow. We have upset the chronology of the despatches in this section to present the visits to cities in the order they occurred, viz., Tashkent, Bukhara, Samarkand, Stalinabad, and Tashkent again (his reports from Frunze and Alma-Ata have not been reproduced).

— January 17, 1955 (Despatch 47) —

At 3 AM on Tuesday, September 21, I flew from the Vnukova airport [at Moscow] for Tashkent to spend a little more than two weeks in Central Asia....

The flight to Tashkent took a little over eleven hours with only one stop — at Aktyubinsk.... [I] found it impossible to sleep on the plane at the height we were flying — over 10,000 feet ... We found ourselves short of breath and when the hostess learned this she spoke to the pilot who said that he could easily fly lower and did so....

I was met at the airport by Mr. Markov, the head of the Intourist agency [the state travel bureau] in Tashkent, and he very efficiently arranged my schedule, bought the plane tickets for the other cities, and telegraphed for reservations at the other hotels....

In the Hotel Tashkent I was given a large two-room suite on the second floor furnished with a grand piano, a large black leather divan, an imposing desk, a table and several chairs, potted ferns, a three-foot high porcelain vase with a picture of Venus and Cupid, a large bronze statue of St. George and the Dragon on a small table, and in one corner of the living room a wash-basin with a cold-water tap which worked but had no plug. (The single tap and the absence of a plug are apparently standard features and were repeated in all the hotels I stayed in with the exception of the one in Bukhara which had no running water.) The small bedroom, separated from the living room by bright red plush drapes, contained two single iron beds covered with natural silk spreads in what I later found to be the traditional colours and patterns of the Uzbeks, a small bedside table with a lamp, and a large wardrobe.

If the toilets had been as good as the room, there would have been little to complain about, but it was rather a shock to discover that in the best hotel in a city of over a million ... the sanitary facilities were extremely primitive: instead of toilet seats, two large foot-shaped cement blocks on the floor at an appropriate angle and not even, as in French institutions of this type, a railing to hang on to. A rusty chain hung down from a rusty reservoir and sometimes it worked and sometimes it did not. At least in this hotel there were women attendants who kept the place passably clean, and it is perhaps enough to say that it was one of the least objectionable I encountered on the trip....

After dinner in the hotel restaurant (standard Soviet fare) I went for a walk. It was the first time I had been in a city which depended entirely on irrigation for its trees and flowers and it was strange at first to see narrow, deep canals along both sides of every street and hear the water gurgling through them. On the asphalted streets the canals were neatly built of cut stone but on the less important streets, some of them still cobbled, the water flowed along in open ditches and sometimes gave off a rather mouldy smell.... It seems to be almost impossible to get grass to grow in these regions but the whole city was green with trees and shrubs and the squares and parks were luxuriant with flowers. Except on the pavements it was always dusty under foot — like clay roads at home in midsummer — and, at least at this time of year, the trees too, were covered with dust; but they were still beautiful and the shade they cast along every street — sometimes in double and triple rows — was very welcome in such a hot climate.

Not far from the hotel was a typical Soviet Park of Rest and Culture for which there was an admission charge of 50 kopecks [about 15 cents Canadian in 1954]. It had the standard equipment — open air theatres and movies, a paved dancing square, places for open-air concerts, shooting booths, outdoor restaurants, a basket-ball court, billiard rooms, chess rooms, etc.

Outside a restaurant near the entrance I got into conversation with some students from the Railway Institute who were climbing over the high iron fence in preference to paying the entrance fee.... when they heard that I was a diplomat from Canada they seemed to be even more eager to talk. They had all had two years of either English or German but had not absorbed much more than we do at home in the same length of time and had of course had no practice in speaking. They had completed the standard ten-year course and were now in the first year at the Railway Institute. When I asked if they would like a glass of beer or lemonade, they said that they would prefer just to talk and spread out a newspaper on a bench. They asked many questions about Canada, the United States and Europe but obviously regarded the prospect of ever seeing anything outside the Soviet Union as very remote. Two girls of about the same age on a nearby bench joined in the conversation and one of them showed that she could speak and understand French quite well. None of them seemed in the least uneasy about talking to a foreigner and paid no attention to a militiaman who gave us, it seemed to me, a rather searching look as he sauntered by. The students asked if they could walk back to the hotel with me and persuaded me to go on a little farther and see the new Opera House, called after the great Uzbek poet Navoi. It had been built by the Japanese prisoners of war, they said, and they had done a very fine job. In the centre of a spacious square in front of the theatre was a large fountain lighted from below in constantly changing colours, of which they were particularly proud. They then walked back again to the hotel and reluctantly said good-bye, asking me to take their friendliest greetings to Canada when I returned....

Mr. Markov had asked if I would like to have a guide to take me around the city and I had thought that it might save time. He was a little surprised himself, I think, when the guide turned out to be a well-known Uzbek folk poet, Nazir Akhimich Akhundi.

He had not been too pleased, he confided later, when he had been asked to leave his work to show some foreign diplomat around the city, but when he had found out that I was interested in literature, it had become a pleasure. Our first expedition was to the main bazaar in a car provided (and charged for) by Intourist. As we drove towards the outskirts of the city, Akhundi pointed out various new institutional and factory buildings, to make way for which more and more of the old flat-roofed clay houses were being torn down. This was the only part of the city in which many of them were still left and even here they were rapidly disappearing.

The bazaar was a colourful sight.... It was so crowded with people buying and selling all sorts of odds and ends — clothing, shoes, kitchen utensils, hardware, etc. — that we had to move slowly. There were little grey donkeys everywhere, hitched to small carts or ridden by old bearded men, or boys or girls or even by whole families, for they have incredibly strong backs for their size. Booth after booth was filled with fresh fruits and vegetables — gorgeous grapes, peaches, pomegranates and green figs etc. — all very cheap. Akhundi was anxious that I should sample all their best fruits and was delighted that I had never eaten green figs (inzhiri). He showed me how to break them in two and rub the two halves together so that they seem still softer and juicier.

As we were eating figs at the counter, a woman came up wearing what looked like a thin metal screen over her face. I thought for a moment that she must have some facial disease or deformity but realized that it must be the purdah. I had thought, somehow, that it would look more like an ordinary veil. It was made out of horsehair, Akhundi said, and in addition to looking ugly, it smelt bad, and was a great nuisance to any woman who had work to do. Very few women still wore them, fortunately. (Markov, the Intourist man, said that it was mostly the wealthier families who still clung to this barbaric old custom.) It was not uncommon to see a woman with this curtain thrown back over her shoulders, I discovered later, but I did not see more than half a dozen women in Tashkent wearing the purinzha (veils).

When we returned to the hotel for lunch, Mr. Markov said that he had made arrangements for us to visit the University and Public Library in the afternoon. I suggested to Akhundi that it might be well to go easy on the vodka at lunch, in order to appear respectable in these institutions of learning. He agreed and we ordered only 100 grams each. When this did not seem quite enough, he repeated the order, assuring me that he knew a trick which he often used on his wife that would certainly work on the scholars. At the hotel desk on the way out, he bought a small bottle of perfume, poured some into his hand and rubbed it on his forehead and insisted that I do the same. He always did that before he came home from a drinking party so that his wife would not scold him. The old pedants would never suspect that we had anything stronger than water.

The Intourist car drove us to the scientific department of the University of Tashkent....

By the time we got back to the hotel, it was too late to go to the Library and the appointment was changed to the next morning. I had noticed that the famous Uzbek folk dancer and singer Tamara Khanum, whom

I had heard when she visited Norway with a Soviet cultural delegation in 1953, was giving a concert that evening in a theatre or concert hall on the same street as the hotel and said that I would like to go. Akhundi said that she was an old friend of his and that he would like to accompany me. Mr. Markov, the Intourist man, ordered the tickets and, to my surprise and Akhundi's disgust, sent one of his assistants, a rather stupid young Uzbek, along with us.

I had the feeling that Mr. Markov thought that Akhundi and I were getting on too well together and that the City Committee had not made a very wise choice of guide. Mr. Markov had worked for Intourist in various cities for many years, spoke English fairly well, and was polite and friendly in a professional Intourist way, although more accommodating, intelligent and efficient than many of their representatives. He was a Russian, of course, about 40 years of age, small and slight but quick and energetic. His right arm was paralyzed, probably from childhood, and the first thing one noticed was that he had to shake hands with his left hand. It was not until I was leaving for Frunze, when he came out to the airport with me, that he began to loosen up a little and reveal a human side beneath the professional exterior. He talked a little about his family, about his education (he was a graduate of the Linguistic Institute) and about the different cities in which he had worked. He was passionately fond of music and knew a great deal about it.

Akhundi, the Intourist assistant and I had seats in the front row. Tamara Khanum was in good form and gave an exciting programme of folk songs and dances from many countries — Chinese, Korean, Indian, Spanish, Hungarian, Finnish, Russian, Norwegian and of course Uzbek — and sang all the songs in the original languages. When we went back stage to speak to her in the intermission, I said that I was probably the only person in the audience that night who understood her Norwegian, which was excellent.... She presented me with three beautiful roses and insisted that I sit down. She had to stay on her feet and keep moving a little during the intermission, she said, or her muscles would stiffen....

As we had had no dinner, we had planned to have something to eat when we got back to the hotel but were unable to shake off the Intourist assistant. We sat and talked in my room for a while, but Akhundi refused a drink and the young man said that he neither drank nor smoked. When we went downstairs, Akhundi refused to go into the dining-room, said good-night and went home. I told him the next day that I had gone to bed hungry. So had he, he said, but how could we talk and enjoy ourselves with that fellow hanging around? I did not know whether he complained or not, but after that Intourist left us alone.

The visit to the Public Library the next day was interesting and pleasant. The director, a white-haired, thin-faced Russian of about 60 and one of his assistants, also an old-regime Russian type, received us in the director's office, where we sat around a table on which they had assembled some of the rare books from their collection, including several incunabula [books·printed before the year 1500 AD] (one of them Luther's Bible), of which they were very proud, and for my special benefit a French translation of Captain Vancouver's *Voyage of Discovery to the North Pacific*. When I mentioned some of the old Scandinavian books I had seen in the Lenin Library, they regretted that they had not known of my interest in Scandinavian literature as they also had some rather rare old Icelandic books, among them a 17th century edition of Snorri's prose Edda. When I inquired about Central Asian manuscripts, they said that the most important ones had been transferred to the library of the Oriental Institute in Moscow, where they were safer and more accessible to scholars. The old assistant, with his owlish eyes and funny old-fashioned moustache, was a real bibliophile and very learned. He knew Arabic and Persian well, spoke French, and read English and German. I should like to have longer with him if I ever go back to Tashkent.

I suspect that the Public Library, like the Art Museum in Tashkent, has profited from the sale of large and valuable private collections since the Revolution. The director of the Art Museum, an Uzbek woman of about 35 and herself a painter, made the tour of the collection with us but called on the curator of the Western European part to help with the explanations. She was a Russian woman, well over 50, with an ugly, troll-like face and dyed hair of an improbably reddish hue, but she was extremely well-versed in her subject, spoke concisely and well, and had a good sense of humour. She made sure that we did not miss seeing a French 19th century painting of a husband who had recently returned home and caught his wife with her lover. I said it reminded me of a French cartoon in which the husband was pointing a gun at the lover and the wife was screaming: Don't shoot the father of your children! This delighted her hugely and she kept chuckling over it for the rest of the tour. The dignified director, whose sense of humour was less robust, smiled politely....

I had to leave for Bukhara the next morning but Akhundi gave me his telephone number and asked me to telephone him on my return to Tashkent.

A few further observations from Tashkent are appended....

— ASHKENT — Conversation with the Poet Akhundi —

As soon as Akhundi decided that he liked me ... he began to talk unaffectedly about his life and work. He was born in a village in Samarkand, and his father was a mullah [moslem religious leader]. Both his parents died while he was small, and he was brought up by an aunt. He had always been fond of music — he had developed a style of singing love lyrics to his own accompaniment on a kind of Uzbek guitar which was very popular and much imitated — and had started early to write verses. His subjects were wine, women, roses, and music, "like our old Omar," he said. Occasionally he would recite one of his short lyrics in Uzbek and then translate it into Russian. They were always short and concentrated with charming and ingenious images. He described how he would sometimes have an experience which moved him (usually amorous) and would not be able to sleep. How could he express it? Then suddenly the inspiration would come and he would get up and write the verses into his little book. Had he not published these lyrics? I asked. Oh, no, they would not do for publication now. Perhaps some day — perhaps not until he was dead. But the Communists could say what they liked, he would write no poems about tractors or cotton pickers or any other mechanical contrivances!...

When I returned to Tashkent after visiting Bukhara, Samarkand, and Stalinabad, I called the number he had given me. His wife answered the telephone. She said that her husband had spoken about me, and that she would telephone him at the publishing house and let him know that I was at the Tashkent Hotel. Akhundi had shown me a picture of his wife, a pretty blonde Ukrainian girl, quite a few years his junior. They had a little boy of eight, who required quite a lot of help from his father on his German homework. Akhundi was fond of his wife and proud of her good looks but made no secret of having a roving eye and giving her good reason to be jealous. At the ballet he pointed out a good looking Uzbek dancer who was one of his old flames. As

we were walking back to the hotel, we ran into her waiting on the
street corner for a bus and he introduced me. Unfortunately her husband
was seeing her home.

Akhundi was quite a good-looking Uzbek type, medium height, well
built, dark complexioned with even features, dark wavy hair, fine eyes
and a pleasant smile — except for half a dozen gold teeth, which may
well be an additional attraction to the Uzbek ladies. (He lost some of
them in the stopperless basin in the hotel one day, but fortunately the
plumber was able to recover them.) He was always well dressed and
had several suits of quite good material. People recognized him everywhere he went, whether because of his reputation as a folk poet or as
a Don Juan I could not be sure, but educated Uzbeks and Tadjiks to
whom I spoke in other cities all seemed to know his poetry.

On getting his wife's message that I was at the hotel, he came over
as soon as he could and found me in the dining room. He had been
working very hard all day on the Pushkin book, for which the publishers
were pressing (it was to come out in a large (150,000) cheap popular
edition) and looked completely exhausted. But after a good steak and
plenty of vodka, he felt energetic enough to go to the Opera....

Akhundi had not the slightest interest in politics. He did not seem to
read the papers very carefully and had no desire to talk about international affairs. He did not even mention Peace.... In our peregrina-
tions Akhundi never missed a pretty face and although his wife was
fair, he admired the long (often reaching down to their knees) black
braids of the Uzbek girls. He pointed out several who had their luxuriant
dark tresses woven into forty thin braids instead of the usual two thick
ones; this meant that they were engaged to be married. The rose was
his favourite flower, and although he liked beer and wine, I came to
the conclusion that vodka was his favourite drink. Although he valued
the additional comforts and conveniences which had come with industrialization, he had no interest in factories and not a great deal in the
extensive building operations which were rapidly changing the appearance even of the suburbs. Nor did the efficient new bus and trolley
lines particularly excite him. He always took taxis. Like all Uzbeks,
he was very hospitable and always wanted to pay for everything, but
it was obvious that he had a comfortable income....

— **February 1, 1955 (Despatch 79)** —

...After Tashkent, Bukhara seemed very provincial. The taxi-driver, who had probably been told by the hotel to bring me in from the airport (since he made no charge) drove me and three other passengers at a good clip in his little Pobeda along the long ribbon of cobblestone road, tooting his horn loudly and rudely at the dignified, unhurrying Uzbeks sitting as erect and proud on an assortment of quilts strapped on to the backs of their small fragile-looking donkeys as if they were monarchs on their thrones. The natives in this region seemed the handsomest I saw, especially the older men with their large dark eyes, strong regular features, dark skins, and well-kept beards. This may be simply because so many more of them were wearing the national costume, which is so much more becoming to them than western dress. The women also kept more to their oriental dress here than in other cities, even the younger women and the school girls, and it seemed to go better with their dark complexions and long braids of hair. Those who preferred to deck themselves and their small children in purple plush from head to foot were more conspicuous but less attractive....

The entrance to ... the hotel was most impressive and I soon found out that it was an old madrasah [a Moslem school] which had been converted into a hotel. Just inside the high pointed archway leading into a large square courtyard, I was met by a rather grubby young man in a peaked cap who said that he had a telegram about me from Intourist in Tashkent. (Some of the service attachés who have visited Bukhara said that he was not the manager of the hotel, as he appeared to be, but an MVD man who took over when there were foreign visitors. He offered to get a guide for me but I refused and saw him only once or twice after that.)....

There was no running water in the room. When you wanted to wash, you took your soap, towel, toothbrush, etc. and walked down the outside stairway and across the courtyard to the umyvalnik [washing room], where there were two zinc troughs filled with cold but beautifully soft water.... The toilets were outside the courtyard through an arch at the back and although primitive were clean.

The ... courtyard had a wide gravel walk all around it. A smaller square in the centre was filled with trees and shrubs.... tables were set under the trees and ... three or four rather slatternly Russian girls were serving meals in the courtyard from a makeshift kitchen. What would

I like to eat, one of them finally got around to enquiring without much interest. Something light, I said, perhaps sliced tomatoes. They had no tomatoes. An omelette perhaps? They had no omelette. What had they? They had only lamb ragout. Then, of course, I would like some lamb ragout and beer. They had no beer. Just tea then. They had no tea. How about coffee? They had no coffee. Well, what had they? They had only lemon sok (a sweetish soft drink flavoured with lemon).

The lamb ragout, I thought, might be good, for lamb is the main meat in Central Asia, but the tousy-headed waitress slapped down in front of me a large plate filled with the toughest chunks of mutton and the soggiest rice I have ever tried to eat. She also brought a plate of brown bread cut in enormous cubes, which at least was very filling. Although there were beautiful melons of all kinds and many other fruits being sold everywhere in the streets, they never had any in the hotel. After one meal in the attractive courtyard, I ate mainly in other restaurants, which were not quite so bad, or bought fruit and the native scones and pirozhki [small meat-, rice- or cabbage-filled dough balls fried or baked] in the streets. In the evenings good tea was served in the hotel.

The most amusing guests were some moving picture people from Moscow, who were making a film about the Revolution in Bukhara and the expulsion of the last Emir [Mohammedan prince]. I was surprised one morning to find a big Rolls-Royce of ancient vintage purring softly in front of the entrance to the madrasah-hotel. It had belonged to the Emir ... I was told, and was now a museum piece. It had been lent by the State for the making of the film. While I was in Bukhara, they were filming inside a kind of kremlin [fortification] on a high hill surrounded by a stout wall. I stood for a time with a great many other curious people in the hot sun outside the huge iron gateway watching the black smoke roll over the tops of the mosques and palaces while men, women and children in colourful native costumes ran about in panic, carrying all sorts of bags and bundles. Every time the gates opened to let a truck or car go in or out, a bunch of boys would force their way into the citadel in spite of the efforts of the militiamen and others to keep them out, but I did not like to make such an unorthodox entry.

As I stood watching, I got into conversation with two teachers — an Uzbek man of about 40, who was teaching mathematics in the Pedagogical Institute, and a blonde Russian girl of about 25, who was teaching the Uzbeks Russian. I do not know whether they were man and wife or not. I was told in Central Asia that Russian men seldom married Uzbek women but that many Russian women married Uzbek men. The girl was very serious and probably a Komsomol [member of the Communist party youth league]. She wanted to know if I had visited the Lenin-Stalin Mausoleum. Although I did not much like looking at corpses, I said, I had been twice — once in 1950 and again last summer. I supposed that she had been. No, unfortunately. When she was in Moscow on a visit a few months ago, she had tried to get a permit and had failed. She had been terribly disappointed, she said, and added with complete sincerity: "How sad it is that such a great and good man as Stalin would have to die!" I was not prepared for that one and muttered something vague about everybody having to die sometime. The man said nothing....

On the movie lot the "Emir of Bukhara" in a gorgeous figured silk gown and turban, a tall stout man with a black beard and heavy make-up, was sitting in an open carriage with no horses. A rough looking red-headed, red-bearded proletarian came up and leaned on the carriage and they carried on an animated dialogue which I could not hear. Then the director shouted through his megaphone, "Vnimanie, Vnimanie!" (attention) and a moment later "poshli!" (action). Smoke poured out and the people in the houses on the wall ran hither and yon for several minutes. This scene was repeated over and over again. The actors' make-up ran in the hot sun and had to be renewed. The director got very angry because some of the boys were talking while the filming was going on and ordered the lot cleared. I went out with the rest. In the evening at the hotel one of the actresses said that she had seen me on the lot. I said that I had found it very interesting but had been chased out. Why had I not come to her and asked to stay, she wanted to know. It was only those noisy boys who were disturbing the work, and they would have been delighted to have me stay as long as I liked.

The film people were a jolly group and sat drinking wine or tea and singing beautifully song after song in four part harmony until the early hours of the morning. Even after that they did not seem to sleep, but wandered around the courtyard in the moonlight talking and laughing. There must have been about thirty of them at the hotel and others were probably quartered elsewhere. One evening they all went off in buses. They were having a party somewhere, a big Georgian in the company told me. They came back very late in high spirits and would certainly have wakened everybody in the hotel, if all the dogs in Bukhara had not been barking all night long in any case....

Most of the inhabitants still live in one-storey clay-covered brick houses with flat clay roofs. Most of the streets are wide enough only for small carts drawn by donkeys, and one wonders how people can find their way home through such a maze. They are very badly lighted at night and as I wandered through them in the darkness and heard the murmur of conversation from small groups of citizens who could not be seen, I thought how easy it would be to knife and rob a passing tourist, but there was not the slightest sign of violence or disorder....

These small clay houses had no windows on the street side. There was just a small door opening into a good-sized courtyard. Mostly the doors were kept shut but I had occasional glimpses into the yards. The houses had windows facing on the court and there were always animated groups of women and children. I was told that the old custom of having no windows on the street side was partly for protection but mainly so that the women of the family were not exposed to the public view as they went about their household activities.

As I was walking through a maze of these narrow streets one day, I was surprised to see a small clay dome above one of the buildings bearing a large sign in black letters: Baptist Temple. I walked around it without managing to find the entrance, which may have been from some courtyard, but I was told by natives that there was quite a large old Baptist community in Bukhara. Whether they are converts from Mohammedanism or from the Greek Orthodox religion, I do not know, but I should guess that they are mainly Russian....

The population of Bukhara was about 50,000, the Russian [a man Watkins met in the park] thought, and very mixed. There was the old Jewish colony which still occupied its own quarter in the city. (I was sorry not to have long enough to investigate.) There were many Russians and Ukrainians and since the Korean war, a large number of North Koreans had been settled there. (I had noticed some of them in the streets and taken them for Chinese.)....

[The next evening, Watkins attended the closing night of the season in the Park of Culture and Rest]

...I took a taxi to the Park. As I walked up the long avenue from the entrance to where the festivities were going on, I met a young Russian and an Uzbek trying to take a drunken Russian friend home. He kept throwing himself on to the ground, rolling in the dust, groaning as if in pain and using very strong language. When the others tried to help him, he attacked them as viciously as he could. Most of the visitors to the Park walked by without paying any attention but a few more boys came to the assistance of the first two and presumably over-powered him and took him home. A few respectable citizens muttered about hooliganism.

The centre of the Park was like a fair with booths selling ice-cream and soft drinks, lepyoshki and pirozhki, grapes and melons, etc. People were dressed in their best, some in national costume, some in purple plush, but most in modern clothes of the type one sees in Moscow. The older Uzbeks, many with small children, seemed to be most attracted by a concert of Uzbek music. Several hundred were seated on chairs and benches under the trees in front of a small platform on which several Uzbek musicians were playing on their weird old instruments for the singers and dancers. A crowd of younger people were standing around the edge and I joined them. They noticed that I was foreign and gladly did their best to explain the subjects of the songs and dances which were giving such obvious pleasure to the large audience.... the most popular artist was a plump young lady who sang love songs and comic numbers in a deep throaty voice and had to give many encores.

Two young working men who had chatted pleasantly at the concert suggested that I go with them to the dance floor. An eight piece orches-tra was playing modern dances and most of the teen-agers were there. My friends knew many of them and while they danced I sat on a bench and talked to anybody who happened to come along. The chauffeur who had driven me from the airport recognized me and introduced a friend. They were both Russian and felt superior to most of the natives because they had been with the army in Germany, Hungary and Czech-oslovakia and could talk knowledgeably about Berlin, Budapest and Prague. Both had had a glass too many and did not mind admitting that they had thoroughly enjoyed life abroad....

The young man whose school-friend I had met on the plane [to Bukhara] had joined us by this time. He knew the two men whose acquaintance I had made at the concert and used that as an excuse for getting into conversation. His father, now dead, had been Uzbek, he said; his mother was Russian. He and his brothers and sisters had grown up speaking both languages. If he had not said that he was Uzbek — his name was Shamir Khakimov — I would have taken him for Russian. Although only 18, he was about six feet tall and broad in proportion with fair hair, blue eyes and Slavic features, but rather dark skin. He was completing the ten-year course next summer and hoped to study architecture in Moscow.

When it began to get chilly, I decided to go home and the three men walked back to the hotel with me. As they were asking questions about various western cities — New York, London, Paris, Rome, Stockholm etc. — one suddenly asked if I had ever been to Tel-Aviv. I had not, but wanted to go because I had several friends there. "Oh, you have friends there?" he repeated, and I said that I had heard a good deal about the interesting new developments in Israel from them. Only then did it occur to me that they might be members of the Bukhara Jewish colony. On saying good-bye a little nervously at the hotel entrance, they said that their names were Yasha Leviev and Ilya Israelov.

They were all sorry to learn that I had not been able to get into the museum in the citadel because it had been closed on account of the filming operations. It would certainly be open the next morning, a Sunday, and I would have time to visit it before the plane left for Samarkand. Ilya said that he would call at the hotel for me at ten o'clock and take me over.

He came to the hotel on his bicycle at the time specified but seemed rather nervous. I said that since I was leaving that day, I wanted to pay my hotel bill before going out. Whether he misunderstood what I said or whether he simply decided that the hotel was a dangerous place for him to be, I do not know, but by the time I came out of the office he had disappeared without a trace. When I went down to the main street to get something to eat, I met Shamir and told him that Ilya had called to take me to the museum but had not waited. Shamir then offered to go out to the museum with me and we took a bus....

The two men we had talked to the night before, Shamir confirmed, were members of the old Bukhara Jewish colony....Shamir came out in the taxi to the airport with me, helped to carry my bags, and waited until the plane left. He very reluctantly accepted 25 roubles to pay his way back to the city....

— January 17, 1955 (Despatch 45) —

[Watkins flew from Bukhara to Samarkand on September 26, and stayed at the city's main hotel, the Registon. After unpacking, he went to the hotel restaurant for a meal.]

She [the head waitress] placed me alone at a table for four at one end of the room. As the restaurant began to fill up, many Soviet citizens asked if the other three places were taken. I always said no, please sit down, but in a few minutes a waitress would come along and move them to another table. It began to get rather comic and people at other tables would smile and wink at me as new candidates for the vacant places approached. Finally, the room got very full and the waitresses gave up and allowed a well-dressed Uzbek to sit at my table. He was a medical doctor of 35 from Tashkent who had just completed five years' service as a naval surgeon in Tallinn, the capital of Estonia. He had not learned Estonian because most of the people he had had to deal with spoke Russian. His wife was a Russian journalist and had been working in Leningrad while he was in Estonia. He had decided that he wanted to practise as a surgeon in Tashkent and his wife also wished to live in Central Asia. The climate was so much better than in Leningrad or in the Baltic countries.

I spent the first evening in a large Park of Rest and Culture not far from the hotel. As it was a Sunday evening, the Park was very crowded and all sorts of entertainments were in progress. The people were better dressed and less provincial-looking than in Bukhara but as there, the teen-agers predominated and the dance-floor was the most popular spot. There were quite a few beggars, most of them young but crippled, some armless, some blind, some legless but moving along swiftly on wheels. A citizen took the trouble to tell me that I should not give them anything as they were war veterans with adequate pensions and only wanted extra money to get drunk. I said that I did not blame them much, for without their limbs they probably never really felt completely well and wanted to forget their troubles for a while. He admitted that there might be something in that. Even people who do not approve in principle of begging usually give something, often accompanying the gift with a short homily. Many war cripples in Central Asian cities have small, specially built automobiles, which are the envy of all the small boys.

A large crowd was listening to a concert of Uzbek music and applauding heartily. An Uzbek youth insisted on sharing a bag of dried sun-flower seeds with me and informed me that this was the only kind of music that the Uzbeks really liked. They could broadcast all the Russian popular songs they liked on the radio but nobody would listen. I ended the evening by going to the last performance of the circus on the grounds. It was a family affair — a man and his wife and brother

— and it must be admitted that they were amazingly versatile....

... [The next day] I decided to see the New Town first and walked for miles along the wide, tree-lined boulevards with their gurgling irrigation channels, to which I had by this time become quite accustomed. Many of the streets were asphalted and there were few of the old mud houses in this part of the city. There were many factories and institutional buildings and a good many large but not very tall apartment houses....

When I got tired walking, I sat down on a bench under a tree in a small park to eat some excellent green lady-finger grapes that I had bought for almost nothing from a street vendor. A little Uzbek boy of about two had helped himself to a bunch about half his own size but when the vendor went to take it from him he set up such a howl that he was allowed to keep it. I had chosen the bench I sat down on because there was a bright-eyed old man sitting there who looked as if he might be interesting to talk to. It was not hard to get into a conversation with him and when he heard who I was he respectfully took off his battered black felt hat, bowed low, shook hands and said that he was greatly honoured. He was clean-shaven and white-haired with strong regular features, a pleasant smile, and twinkling blue eyes behind dark-rimmed spectacles. He was 75, he said, and had seen quite a lot in his time. He had been twice in jail — never for anything criminal, of course, always political — and he had just got out a few months ago. While he was "sitting," people had stolen all his books and clothes. The things he was wearing were all "government." He was a native of Kazan. He had been sent to jail the first time just after the Revolution and when he got out had been exiled to Samarkand. His wife had come with him but she had died some years ago. He had two children, a son and a daughter, living in Moscow and doing well but they never did anything to help him. He saw little of them and did not regret it. If he had his life to live over again, he would remain a bachelor.

The last jail sentence had been for stealing money from the institution where he was employed as a bookkeeper. He had been perfectly honest, of course, and the evidence of that was that he was employed again as a bookkeeper now. He had had millions of roubles passing through his hands and had never taken any but had been the goat for the knavery of others. However, in jail he had had time to do a lot of reading and develop a philosophy and he could take anything they chose to give without getting in the least upset about it. And he spat vigorously to show how little he cared.

In all the years he had lived in Samarkand he had never learned more than a few words of Uzbek. They were just trash (dryan), these people, and he had no use for them. They were lazy and shiftless. Some of the women might be attractive, with their long black braids and black eyes, but they were stupid and backward. They were married young to older men and although they were carefully watched and knew that if they were caught they would probably be knifed, they were always ready to cheat their husbands when they got the chance. Now the Uzbeks were supposed to be educated and they were professors of this, that and the other, but he had no faith in their learning. It was just a bluff. These Communists were just bluffers anyway — ignorant upstarts. Life in Kazan before the Revolution — that was something! He had known both Gorki and Chaliapin. Both were gifted, of course, but both were alcoholics. He had no use for Gorki as a writer. He never read any of these moderns. Give him Pushkin, Dostoyevsky, Tolstoy — that was literature. As for Central Asians, he would never dream of reading anything they could write. They were just trash, the lot of them.

[The next day Watkins was joined for lunch].

... at about eleven o'clock, an Uzbek sat down at my table in the restaurant and ordered soup, pickled cucumbers, and cognac. As I was drinking only Tashkent mineral water, he insisted that I share his cognac. He had a square, pale brown face with strong jaw bones, small bright black eyes, and rather coarse black hair. He looked as if he might have Mongolian blood, and the people in this region are so mixed that it is not improbable that he had. He had been left an orphan at an early age, he told me later, and had been brought up in a State institution. He was short and stocky with large heavy hands, and looked like a peasant, except that he was well dressed in a light coloured shirt and brown suit of good material. He was about 40....

His name was Abdullah.... His wife was a Tadjik and they had six children — two boys and four girls....

[Watkins accepted an invitation by Abdullah to join him at home for an authentic regional meal prepared by his wife.]

... She had prepared two special Central Asian dishes — monty (chopped meat wrapped in a paste and boiled, something like the Siberian pyelmeni, and served with sour cream) and ploff (pilaff). [Abdullah] followed the beer with vodka, in which a number of toasts had to be drunk, and we drank a sweet native wine with the dessert (cake and ice-cream). They could not have been more friendly and hospitable and when I left, they walked back to the hotel with me. There [Abdullah] decided that we should have coffee and cognac to top things off.

After that they came up to my room. [Abdullah's wife] had not drunk anything but he was a little unsteady on his feet and I was so tired that I could hardly keep my eyes open. They sat down on one of the beds and he told me in a stage whisper that he just wanted to let me know that he was with us and against the Communists. What was more, he was not alone. He had many friends who thought just as he did, and not only in Uzbekistan, not only in Central Asia, but in many parts of the country. But what could they do? The Americans would have to give a great deal more economic assistance if they expected results. [Abdullah's wife] was too much a Muslim wife to express any disapproval of what her husband was saying, but I thought she was looking rather nervous. She made my obvious weariness an excuse for dragging him home. I had begun to wonder if he might be an angent provocateur and had confined my remarks to a sleepy "Yes, yes. I understand." He finally left, saying that he would be aroudn at ten o'clock in the morning to see me off.

He came into my room when I was having tea the next morning looking very subdued and contrite. He was afraid he had been a little drunk last night and might have said some things he shouldn't. I said that I had been a little drunk too and did not remember what he had said and he made no further reference to the subject.

Although I had already spent some time in the swarming bazaar, I wanted to go again and buy some souvenirs. [Abdullah] was only too pleased to accompany me and was of some help in shopping: when a young Uzbek merchant asked 130 roubles for a beaded tibiteika [Moslem skull cap], he said something in Uzbek which reduced it immediately to 65. An Uzbek who had seen us looking at the bead-work came up as we were leaving and told us that he was a "master" in that profession and had done a portrait of Stalin in beads which we might like to see; his house was just around the corner from the market. I supposed he wished to sell the picture, but it appeared that he only wanted us to look at it. I was glad of the chance to see the inside of one of the old-style clay houses ([Abdullah's] was modern with windows facing on the street and no courtyard.) This one was windowless on the street side and the entrance was from a small courtyard on which were three or four other small dwellings. There was no door into the living-room — just a curtain covering the opening. It was not very large but was fairly well lighted from windows on the court. The only furniture, except for rugs and piles of quilts, was the table at which the master worked, a chair, and a powerful electric light. The picture was hanging on the wall above the table. It was a good likeness of the great leader and teacher in uniform with medals and with touches of bright red on the shoulders. It had taken the master two solid years, for in order to get the proper shading with all the thousands of tiny glass beads, he had had to work at night under artificial light. We admired the portrait from all angles and insisted on taking it out into the yard so that we could see it in the full daylight. The master was very pleased and invited us to drink tea with him but unfortunately there was not time....

[Abdullah] came out to the airport with me in a taxi....

As the plane was late, we had plenty of time for shashlik and beer in the vine-covered open-air restaurant at the airport. In fact we went around to the side where the chef was preparing shashlik on a charcoal brazier and were assured that it would take only a few minutes. In speaking of his children, [Abdullah] said that he was worried because the two little boys, now six and three, had not yet been circumcised. The custom was to have a great feast and invite all your friends but the Communists were against it and he did not know quite what to do. I asked if it could not be done without so much publicity but apparently the operation without the elaborate feast and ceremonial is not satisfactory.

— January 14, 1955 (Despatch 35) —

Late in the afternoon of September 29 I arrived in Stalinabad [now called Dushanbe] after an uneventful two-hour flight ... This was a part of the journey which the Ministry has said that I would not be permitted to make by train, because the railway went through a restricted zone. There were no taxis at the airport and when I ordered one through Intourist three amiable Russian engineers who had arrived by the same plane asked if they could have a ride with me to the hotel. I did not want them to pay, as I would have had to pay the same amount for the taxi if I had ridden alone, but they insisted and the chauffeur, an Uzbek, settled the matter by announcing what he considered appropriate for each....

Stalinabad is situated in a fertile valley — the Gissarskaya Dolina — and the surrounding mountains, some of them snow-capped, add to its charm. Its rapid growth seems like a miracle to the older inhabitants and the population as a whole seems to be filled with a sense of pride in its achievements. Although the peasants who come in to the bazaars from the hills round about stick to their native costumes and customs, these were less in evidence than in the older cities of Uzbekistan. I saw no women wearing veils, for instance, in the Stalinabad bazaars, although there were many old men wearing turbans who sat cross legged on the ground all day with half a dozen small glasses filled with spices for making ploff in front of them, selling it by the spoonful, and a great many young, able-bodied men drinking tea by the hour in the chaikhanas [tea rooms] when one would have thought they could be better employed harvesting cotton....

— Stalinabad — Conversation with Students —

[Watkins met a group of students who offered to show him around the city's university. One of them, Khalek Abdu, may have become the homosexual plant in the plot to ensnare Watkins in Moscow.]

The student who spoke first was an Uzbek named Khalek Abdu. As we walked along he introduced his friends. I have forgotten their names, but there was a Tadjik, a Pamir, a Russian, a Ukrainian and a Jew in the group and they were specializing in various fields. The Uzbek remarked on the many nationalities in the group and said that this was typical not only of the university but of the city. The university like all the other large buildings in Stalinabad, was only a few years old but it was already overcrowded. A long, plain, ell-shaped, light-coloured, two storey building, it was set well back from the tree-lined boulevard....

... Some of the group who had come with me had disappeared but other students had joined us and were asking all sorts of questions....

Didn't Canada belong to the aggressive Atlantic Pact [NATO], one aggressive young man wanted to know. It was a defensive not an aggressive alliance, I replied. Defensive against what, they wanted to know. Against any country that might be strong enough to attack, I replied. Then surely it must be obvious that the Soviet Union stood for peace and had no intention of attacking any other country. I said that since the [February 1948] coup in Czechoslovakia in which a Communist minority had taken over the government, many other European countries were afraid of their own Communist parties attempting something similar and they did not want Communist revolutions any more than they wanted war.

... Khalek, the Uzbek, had still so many questions to ask that he walked the streets with me for a couple of hours. He was very young, only eighteen, and in his first year in economics.... He was tall and thin with a round brown face, large dark eyes and unruly black hair. He was plainly but well dressed in a dark turtle-neck sweater and suede sports jacket. Although he had been born in Stalinabad, his parents were both Uzbek and he was, he said, of almost pure Arab blood. His people were evidently well enough off that he had never had much to do but study, and no matter how excited he got about the subject under discussion he was always extremely polite.

Khalek's ambition had always been to enter the diplomatic service and he had thought of going directly into the diplomatic training school in Moscow — if only he could get in. The competition was very keen. Then he had decided that it would be better to take a degree in economics first, so that if he did not succeed in getting into the diplomatic service ... he would have his economics training to fall back on. In any case, he planned to go to Moscow for post-graduate studies when he had finished the five-year course in Stalinabad. He was determined that he would not marry before 26 or 28, no matter how strong the family pressure might be.... It was considered very bad in that part of the country not to raise a family as soon as possible, but he wanted to finish his studies first.

Could people read the works of Marx and Lenin in Canada, he wanted to know. They could if they wanted to, I told him. Was Marx studied in the universities? Yes, you could hardly give a course in 19th century political and economic thought without Marx, I replied. "But I cannot understand how they can let the students read Marx if they are afraid of Communism," he exclaimed. I said that that was part of what we called our liberal tradition — that people read what they liked and made up their own minds about it. Did they teach Marx in the primary and secondary schools? No, they did not; if a man were a Catholic or a Presbyterian, he taught his children Catholicism or Presbyterianism from the age of three or so. That was a question of religion, and it seemed to me that in the Soviet Union Communism was a kind of religion, which people taught their children to believe in from their earliest years. "A religion," he exclaimed. "But in a religion there is always God." "Well, you have what you think is the one and only truth and that is your substitute for God," I replied. This idea was obviously novel and disturbing and he was not prepared to counter it.

As we walked around the large fountain in front of the Opera, on one side of which was my hotel, he suddenly asked if I knew many people in this city. (I had said that I was hungry and had asked if he would have dinner with me in a small restaurant but he had refused and I had bought pirojki from a street-vendor instead.) I did not know anybody, I said, but of course the people in the hotel knew who I was. He talked about other things for awhile and then abruptly enquired where my body-guard was. I told him that I had none and was travelling quite alone; I could not imagine that anybody wanted to murder me. But Comrade [Andrei] Vishinsky had had a body-guard when he had visited Stalinabad. But he was Vishinsky, I replied, and the Foreign Minister. Well, don't you suppose Mr. [John Foster] Dulles [the American Secretary of State] has a body-guard when he travels? he asked. He probably had, I said, but he was a very important man. Khalek thought ambassadors were important people too and would all have body-guards, but I assured him that none of the ambassadors I knew in Moscow had any. I hope I did not disillusion him with the profession.

Like all intelligent young Soviet citizens, Khalek was avid for outside contacts and thrilled at the mere idea of travelling abroad. He asked innumerable questions about Canada and when I showed him pictures from the farm [at Norval Station, Ont.], he thought the countryside looked very beautiful. Maybe he would come and visit me on my farm in Canada some day, he said daringly. I assured him that he would be most welcome. Wouldn't he be arrested because he came from the Soviet Union? Not if he came on a proper visa, I said.... The old brick farm house struck him as very large and he said he supposed I must be some kind of aristocrat. On the contrary, I said, I was a peasant or at most a kulak [well-to-do peasant]. He looked around, as if to make sure that nobody had heard, and laughed.

Khalek just loved American jazz, he said, and all the students listened to it on the radio. I admitted that I was not a fan. But it was so wonderful to dance to, he said: the rhythms simply made your blood boil. (In general, I imagine, the boiling point of Central Asian blood is low.) It seems clear from this that American musical programmes, perhaps from German stations, are not difficult to hear in Central Asia and are not jammed....

Had I ever heard Paul Robeson [black American singer and actor] sing? Khalek wanted to know. I had heard him several times and had also seen him act the role of Othello. Khalek had not known that he was an actor but he was a marvellous singer and even sang in Russian. He had sung several times in the Soviet Union but according to the papers he was not allowed now to leave the United States. Khalek had read, too, that the Americans had recently suppressed the Communist Party; he supposed it would go underground! Was there a Communist Party in Canada? What were the main political parties in Canada? What was the Government? The Communist parties in Canada, Britain and Scandinavia might be very small, but he knew that they were not so small in France and Italy. How did people live in Canada and in Western Europe? Was there any unemployment? What was a Canadian farm like? Was agriculture highly mechanized? Did we grow much cotton? What kind of grains and fruits had we?...

Khalek said that he felt that he should tell me — and it was of course no secret — that he was a Komsomol and one of the leaders in the university group. This probably made it more risky for him to be seen in the company of a foreigner, and he was clearly a little worried about what people would think. I said that he must not stay with me if he felt that it might be misunderstood. I thought that we both had clear consciences; we were not trying to convert each other; but I would not want him to get into any trouble on my account. He could see no harm in our conversation, he said, and it was so interesting to talk to a foreigner. I suggested that he might have some reading to do for the next day but he said that he had just finished his assignments when he met me at the library and had nothing in particular to do for the rest of the evening.

It was getting late when Khalek reluctantly said good-bye and got on to his trolley. Before leaving, he wrote his name and address in my little book and said he hoped he would hear from me. I sent him a postcard from Paris but have had no reply, although cards from Paris to a friend in Tashkent and another in Stalinsk have been cordially acknowledged.

Interlude,
October, 1954 to March, 1955

Watkins here details the so-called Burmese incident, in which he and six other ambassadors walked out of a dinner party because diplomats for several countries not recognized by the West were also to attend. The wire services were quick to seize upon the story, and it found its way into many Canadian newspapers. The head of the British Labor Party at the time, Dr. Edith Summerskill, labelled the walkout "boorish and clumsy." It is clear, though, that Watkins had little choice in the matter after having been duped by the Burmese Ambassador.

— October 19, 1954 (Despatch 662) —

On returning from Central Asia I found that a telephone invitation from the Burmese Ambassador, Mr. Maung Ohn, for an informal dinner at the Sovietskaya Hotel had been accepted for me and confirmed by a little note which read as follows: "Dear Colleague, I am glad to know that I shall have the pleasure of your company at a dinner on Monday, the 18th October, 1954, at the Restaurant of the Sovietskaya Hotel, Leningrad Shosse 44/2, at 8:30 PM. I am looking forward to the occasion. Yours sincerely, Maung Ohn." This seemed slightly peculiar, since the normal practice is to send a pour memoire card, but the Burmese Ambassador prides himself on not only his humility but also on his unconventionality. He always entertains at hotels and it did not occur to me that this would be anything but an ordinary diplomatic matter.

At a luncheon here on the day of the dinner, Mrs. Thorsteinsson, the wife of the Icelandic Minister, said that her husband had been invited in the same way but that she had not been invited. It was obviously to be a dinner only for men and only for heads of mission and she suspected that the Burmese was taking advantage of his position as acting dean of the corps, in the absence of the Swedish Ambassador, to invite together all the heads of mission in Moscow, including the Chinese, North Korean, Viet Minh, Outer Mongolian, Albanian and East German....

I assumed that if he had invited all heads of mission it would be like the receptions at the satellite embassies which always include the representatives of countries which we do not recognize and at which one sees but does not meet them. However, when I arrived at the Sovietskaya Hotel, I saw the American Ambassador standing on the sidewalk waiting for his car. A few minutes later the Dutch, British and Greek Ambassadors came out of the hotel on their way home.

They had told the Burmese that they had noticed that representatives of countries which they did not recognize were present and that they were sure that he would understand in the circumstances why they could not stay. He had said that he was sorry but understood their position. (The Greek Ambassador had noted that on the seating plan he was beside the East German Ambassador.)

The Norwegian Ambassador, who had arrived in the meantime, and I decided that we would go in also and explain to Mr. Ohn why we did not feel that we could stay. We solemnly checked our coats in the garderobe and went into the reception room. Fortunately he was standing near the door and met us before we had to speak to anybody else. With his usual saccharine smile, he said that it was not clear to him why a sitting-down dinner should be different from the kind of buffet supper at which we were often present with all heads of mission in Moscow, but that if we felt that we should not stay, he would understand. As we were putting on our coats, he came out and shook hands again and assured us that he understood.

The Norwegian came home with me for a drink and about ten o'clock the Dutch Ambassador telephoned to say that all the évadés [escapees] were assembled at the Belgian Embassy and to suggest that we join them. (Some of the uninvited wives had been having a consolation dinner there.) The Belgian Ambassador returned a little later, and we went into another room to discuss the situation — the United States, United Kingdom, French, Dutch, Norwegian and Belgian Ambassadors and myself.

It was only then that I learned that Mr. [Viacheslav] Molotov [the Soviet Foreign Minister] had also been present. Nobody was much concerned about the Burmese Ambassador's feelings, but nobody wished to seem disrespectful to the Foreign Minister. It was agreed that either a personal letter to Mr. Molotov or a call on the Chief of Protocol, Mr. Kiselyov, to explain the situation would be in order. On the suggestion of the American Ambassador, who had smelt a rat, the Swiss Chargé, Mr. de Stoutz, had called on the Burmese Ambassador a few days earlier to enquire about the composition of the dinner and the Burmese had simply refused to answer. It was felt, therefore, that the dinner had been arranged as a kind of trap and that even if we had been told in advance that the Foreign Minister would be present we should still not have wished to attend. The Greek Ambassador and I thought we would prefer to call on the Chief of Protocol.... The others were writing Molotov this morning. It seemed better also that all should not follow the same course and that the letters of those who wrote should not be uniformly worded.

At about 11:30, the Icelandic Minister and the Swiss Chargé, whose wives had been dining at the Belgian Embassy, came in with reports of the dinner. Mr. Ohn, with tears in his voice, had spoken in Russian of his wish to bring people together and quoted the old Russian proverb: "Mountains do not meet but people meet." The empty places showed that his attempt had not been entirely successful. But we were all human beings, etc. Molotov, who as Mr. de Stoutz remarked is no cretin and clearly understood the situation, thanked the Burmese Ambassador for his "initiative" and good intentions. He mentioned that all would be meeting again on November 7 and many times after that, he hoped. It was obviously his intention, Mr. de Stoutz thought, to console the Burmese a little but glide over the incident lightly. The Argentine Ambassador praised Mr. Molotov's efforts in the cause of peace. [Deputy Premier Mikhail] Pervukhin uttered some banalities about peace. The Luxembourg Minister, Mr. Blum, made what Mr. de Stoutz said could only be understood as a passionate declaration of love to the Soviet Union and to Mr. Molotov. He had now been in this country for ten years, but he had grown younger. He was pleased to note that Mr. Molotov was also growing younger. It was a country of youth and enthusiasm. They would all drink to Mr. Molotov as the great peace-maker, etc. He spoke in Russian and then summarized his remarks in French and English. His face, Mr. de Stoutz said, radiated joy but as he continued, his speech became increasingly ridiculous. Mr. Molotov began to smile very early and by the end it had become so grotesque that almost everybody was laughing. Mr. Thorsteinsson said that it was highly embarrassing and he had felt like getting up and walking out.

Mr. de Stoutz said that he was sure that Mr. Molotov had known the composition of the guest list. Mr. Bohlen, who was considerably upset over the whole business, began to reconsider whether, if Mr. Molotov was a party to the trick, he should write to him or not. I said that my guess would be that Mr. Molotov had been informed that all heads of mission had accepted Mr. Ohn's invitation but that he probably did not know that Mr. Ohn had not told the Western diplomats that he was inviting the East German etc. or that he was inviting the Foreign Minister himself, for that matter. If Molotov had known this, he would surely have foreseen difficulties and it is fairly certain that the Russians wish to avoid embarrassments of this kind just now. I suspected the Holy Ohn of having cheated on both sides....

By an odd coincidence I had an appointment to call on the Burmese Ambassador this morning.... As could be expected, I found him armed in saintliness and seraphic smiles.... I mentioned that I was going to Paris on Friday to meet the Minister [for External Affairs, Lester Pearson]. He seemed to take it for granted that I was going to be fired and spoke consolingly about the Higher Life. I had a feeling from the general tenor of his lofty incoherence that he had spent a good part of the night wondering whether he would be recalled for his exploit or not and persuading himself that he really did not care....

... I have seen the Chief of Protocol, Mr. Kiselyov, who received me with Mr. Teplov, formerly Soviet Chargé d'Affaires in Ottawa....

I ... said that I wished to refer briefly to the embarrassing incident of the evening before in connection with the Burmese Ambassador's dinner and explained the circumstances of the invitation and my reasons for leaving. It was only later that I learned that the Foreign Minister had been present. There had also been other high officials, Mr. Kiselyov said, including Mr. Pervukhin and Mr. [Ivan Fyodorovich] Tevoysyan. It seemed to me that when the Burmese Ambassador invited the Foreign Minister and other high officials he should have informed his other guests. Quite a few had stayed for the dinner, Mr. Kiselyov remarked. Yes, and some of them had felt pretty uncomfortable, I added. Mr. Kiselyov merely looked uncomfortable himself, and I suspect that he may have had a chilly morning interview with his chief. I made it clear that no disrespect for the Foreign Minister had been intended and left it to Mr. Kiselyov to convey this to the Foreign Minister or not as he saw fit....

In the fall of 1954, Watkins made the acquaintance of an historian at the Ministry of Education, Nikolai Andreyev. The two first met on the plane back to Moscow following the ambassador's trip through the Central Asian republics, by which time he had opened himself to blackmail. The secret police, who knew about the incidents and were laying a trap, may have enlisted Andreyev to help with the scheme. He sat beside Watkins in the plane and their mutual interest in history sparked a conversation. Andreyev is only the first of a suspicious series of new acquaintances who began to cross paths with Watkins after the trip.

— November 30, 1954 (Letter 735) —

Last night I had dinner in the restaurant of the new 26-storey Leningrad Hotel, near the Leningrad station [in Moscow], with Nikolai Ivanovich

Andreyev, historian on the staff of the Ministry of Education. I met him on the plane coming back from Alma-Ata October 6-7. He is in charge of coordinating the work on a series of histories of the Central Asian republics and has to make frequent trips to confer with the historians in the various national academies who are doing the work. He had telephoned shortly after our return to Moscow and I had dined with him at the Aragvi Restaurant on October 14 but had had to leave early to attend the reception for the British parliamentary delegation.

He telephoned again shortly before I left for Paris on October 22 to say that he was off again to Central Asia — Tashkent and Samarkand this time — and to ask if I would like him to bring back any books. I mentioned a book by Tolstov on the archaeological excavations at Khorezm which I had not been able to find in Moscow, and he had it with him last night. I was embarrassed when I heard that he finally had to extract it from the library of an Uzbek professor (it had been published only in 3,000 copies, most of which were in public libraries) but he seemed quite proud of his exploit.

Nikolai gives only his first name over the telephone. He said on the plane that he would do this. When I suggested the possibility of his coming to the Embassy for dinner, he said that he knew we always had policemen on guard at the gate and that it might therefore be better to meet at restaurants. We had not been sitting long at the table in the imposing dining-room of the Leningrad when a young man in spectacles with dark hair and a premature bald spot came up and spoke to Nikolai. He said that he wanted to speak to him privately for a moment and Nikolai excused himself and went a few paces away. He came back laughing and said that the young man, who also worked in the Ministry of Education, had just wanted to warn him that the man sitting at the table with him was the Canadian Ambassador. "You don't say so," Nikolai had exclaimed. "I had no idea I was dining in such distinguished company." The young man said that he would not have known but his friend who had been dining with him had recognized me. Nikolai then explained to the young man that he had met me on a plane and that I had told him right away who I was, so they need not worry. That, I supposed, was what was known as "vigilance."

Nikolai is a widower of about 45. His wife and two small children were killed in the bombing of Rostov-on-the-Don while he was at the front and he can still hardly bear to speak of it. He was an officer, was wounded once and sent to a sanitarium in the Caucasus to convalesce, and spent some time with the Soviet Army in Berlin. His parents were poor peasants in the Rostov region and he would not, he thinks, have had a chance to study if it had not been for the Revolution. He graduated in history from Leningrad University in the Twenties and was a teacher before entering the Ministry. He has read a great deal in English and, although he has had little practice, understands fairly readily and expresses himself clearly if awkwardly. He is eager to improve — and this is one of the main reasons for his telephoning, I think — and has offered to help me with Russian. On the plane he had said that he used to enjoy reading *The New Statesman* and *Nation* and I had taken a couple of copies long for him to the Aragvi. He was delighted when he found that I had brought some more this time and also a couple of detective stories.

In spite of the many hardships of student life in Leningrad in the Twenties, Nikolai has pleasant and piquant memories of his university years. There was a lively intellectual ferment in Leningrad student circles in those days, and practically all the students belonged to one or more of the many student societies which were formed as discussion or social groups and were to say the least highly unconventional. Nikolai had not himself belonged, because of the expense, but he had been to some of their meetings. There was one called the Blue Lamp to which he had gone one evening when he felt that he had five roubles — quite a sum in those days — to spare. The room was furnished only with the table on which the Blue Lamp stood. The students all sat on the floor. But there was plenty of vodka, of course, and the discussion of all sorts of topics gained momentum as the night wore on. At an appropriate time the girls went out and changed into transparent costumes and then performed some more or less oriental dances.

Towards the end of the NEP period,[1] in 1928 and 29, there was a good deal of money in circulation, some of the students came from well-to-do merchant families, and the pace became increasingly hectic. One of the societies was called "The Glass of Water." It was based on the free love theory then prevalent and the idea was that fornication was as simple and natural a process as drinking a glass of water and no questions of morals or conscience were involved. It was a pretty pernicious doctrine, Nikolai thought. A great many very nice intelligent girls from good decent families had "given themselves" to all and sundry and ruined their lives. The poet [Serge] Essenin was a victim of this period of loose living and ended in suicide. In 1929 the brakes were put on and by 1930 there had been a complete transformation....

... [Nikolai] considered countries like Canada and the Scandinavian countries, for instance, genuine democracies. He was not so sure about England. I said that although the division into classes was still very marked in England and showed up in accent, manner, dress, etc., England had in some ways become more socialistic, more of a welfare state, in recent years than even the Scandinavian countries with free medical and dental care, etc. Nikolai said that he thought that it was a great pity that there was not more information available here on recent developments in England....

After dinner, which with the leisurely service of the Leningrad lasted until after midnight, Nikolai rode with me to the corner nearest to his apartment on Kirovskaya Street. It was plain that he felt rather daring riding in a car flying the Canadian flag. He said that he would telephone again.

— February 16, 1955 (Despatch 137) —

[Here, Watkins details some of the confusion in the diplomatic corps surrounding the resignation of Malenkov. It was not at all clear at the time that Khrushchev's star was rising.]

Mr. Malenkov's letter of resignation ... stunned the occupants of the diplomatic boxes and the foreign press boxes when it was read out by the Chairman of the Council of the Union ... on February 8....

When we assembled for the 4:00 o'clock meeting [of the Supreme Soviet], most of the diplomats were wondering whether the successor would be Khrushchev or Molotov, except the Swedish, Norwegian and Austrian Ambassadors, who were betting on Bulganin. [The Swedish Ambassador] Mr. Sohlman arrived at this view, I have been told since, by a process of elimination: Malenkov had spoken in his letter of his lack of ministerial experience; Khrushchev had not had any either; Molotov had had a good deal but he was old and tired and more than busy enough in a post for which there seemed to be no obvious successor; Bulganin had had ministerial experience, was known to be an able administrator, was very popular with the people and was the kind of dignified, fatherly figure, very Russian in every way and even rather old regime in appearance, in whom the people would have confidence if they were to be asked to make further sacrifices either because of increased danger of war or merely to put their national economy on a sounder basis.

When Mr. Khrushchev came to the tribune to make the announcement, everybody understood that it would not be he and the United

States Ambassador is said to have exclaimed: "It can't be Khrushchev, so it must be Molotov." As the British Ambassador remarked, it seemed unlikely that anyone would be writing a despatch beginning, "As I predicted last week." As far as our soundings of popular reactions go, there was great surprise but not great excitement. Many Russians have recalled that Malenkov's health had long been poor; he was said to have a bad heart. The visiting Hearst newspapermen were given a broad hint when they asked for an appointment with Malenkov and were informed that that could not be arranged but that if they could stay until Friday they could have an appointment with Bulganin. As this hardly seemed worth waiting for, they went on to Leningrad on their way home. On hearing that Bulganin had become Prime Minister, they requested an interview, returned to Moscow, and were received on February 12.

— February 22, 1955 (Letter 146) —

[Watkins met the Kazakeviches for a visit to a museum in late January, and afterwards invited them to his apartment at the Canadian Embassy for dinner.]

For some reason there seemed to be quite a bit of conversation about Jews.... [Kazakevich said that] Czarist Russia had never known how to absorb the Jews and make proper use of their abilities. Napoleon had done much better. When he decided to become Emperor, he needed a court. A nobleman to make a good appearance at court needs a pair of pants. So Napoleon had married off his breechless courtiers to the daughters of wealthy Jewish bookers [financiers] and it had worked out very well.

In Nicholas I's time the army had frequently raided Jewish villages and carried off the children to give them a Greek Orthodox education in military academies. It was something like what the Canadian Government seemed to be doing just now, according to what he read in the papers, with the children of the Doukhobour Sons of Freedom who refused to send their children to school, except that Nicholas I's soldiers had often strung the parents up on the nearest trees. But the motive was to save the children and educate them in accordance with the ideas of the autocracy and not of their misguided parents....

Mrs. Kazakevich said that Kazakevich was always making remarks which made her shudder because some people would certainly take them as anti-Semitic. Had I ever known any Jewish people when I was young? Not until I went to university. Neither had she, except some friends of the family, the Omans, of whom they had all been very fond. Her father had been very much opposed to anti-Semitism and proud of his friendship with this family, but when one of her sisters had married a Jew, he had turned around completely and been very bitter that a daughter of his could do such a thing. It had been very disillusioning. She herself had really met very few Jews until after she had graduated from Bryn Mawr and she had been delighted to find what clever, intelligent and charming people they were....

I mentioned an article which had appeared recently in *Soviet Culture* on some of the habits of the young people who drank too much, smashed up the family car, dressed in extreme styles imitated, allegedly, from Western movies which they somehow or other got hold of and showed privately, danced *stilom* (boogie-woogie, apparently) etc. They were called *stilyagi*. Kazakevich had heard the word used among the young people at the Economics Institute. Formerly the "Hamburg" and the "atom" dance had been fashionable; this winter it was the "Canadian." I had no idea what that was; neither had they. It certainly could not be square-dancing, Mrs. Kazakevich said; she had done lots of that in Muskoka and it was good healthy fun.

It was interesting, I thought, to observe that the Soviet authorities were now having to cope here with the problems of affluence. These young people were obviously the children of well-to-do parents, who gave them too much money, let them use their cars, and generally spoiled them. This business with the cars was really getting quite serious, Kazakevich said. It was serious anywhere, I thought. But it was worse here, he said, because so many of the roads were so bad and they drove too fast, wrecked the cars, and injured themselves and others. Many of them were the children of old Party workers who had come to the top by a very hard road. Their whole life had been given over to Party work. They were never at home in the evenings — always at meetings. And they were so used to this kind of life that even if they had no reason to hold a meeting, they invented one, because they simply did not know any other way to live. They practically never saw their children — it was the same with most of the mothers who were also Party workers — and the children got no training at home. Having had such a hard life themselves, the parents wanted their children to have an easier time and kept them too well supplied with money. Then they were surprised when they learned that they were drinking too much, idling their time instead of studying or working, and keeping bad company.

Kazakevich knew of one group of teen-agers who spent a great deal of their time walking up and down Gorki Street, wearing zoot suits and long hair, and addressing each other as ''sir'' in English. They could not speak English, of course; all they knew was a few expressions like ''very good'' and ''how are you?'' but they made the most of them to make ordinary Russians think they were Americans. They always referred to Gorki Street as ''Broad-vay....''

Kazakevich said that social prestige here now depended rather on *where* you worked than on how much you were paid. There might be little or no difference in the salary you could earn in a factory in Zagorsk or in the Foreign Ministry but the difference in prestige was enormous. The Economics Institute was a good stepping-stone to high government positions. Gromyko, for instance, had at one time been a secretary of the Institute. Not long ago one of their young economists had been transferred to Kaganovich's staff, which has its offices in the Kremlin. Although his salary would be about the same, he felt much more important and had left with his nose in the air. ''if there's anything I can do for you, comrades, just give me a ring at the Kremlin.''

It did not seem to me that human nature was changing very rapidly under Marxism; the weakness for alcohol was a good example. Kazakevich said that the amount of hard drinking had shocked him when he came back here from the United States. Did I know what it was like in the big coal and steel cities in the United States? New York was nothing by comparison. And when he had lectured in those cities in which drunkenness was such a problem he had always preached that it was due to the lack of the cultural facilities — workers' clubs offering reading rooms, concerts, plays, etc. — so plentifully supplied in the Soviet Union. Then he had come to live in Molotov ([now called] Perm), a big industrial city in the Urals, and had found to his horror that in spite of all kinds of palaces of culture, cheap concerts and theatres, lending libraries and lectures, the well-paid workers could be found by the dozen not only dead drunk but lying in the ditches along the roads. The pious Marxist, Mrs. Kazakevich, said that she was afraid that that was one respect in which Marxism had failed; the social approach did not seem to work and obviously a more individual approach was needed.

— **March 4, 1955 (Despatch 173)** —

[The Moscow diplomatic community was curious whether Malenkov's downfall would lead to major re-shuffling in the Kremlin. Three weeks after Malenkov's resignation, no such changes had appeared.]

If there is one thing that can be deduced from the recent changes at and near the top here, it is that Soviet politics remain hazardous grounds for predictions. Observers in Moscow had sensed that there was a tug-of-war in the Government and that Malenkov might turn out to be on the short end of it, but nobody here today is able to claim that he had expected the denouement to come at the time it came or in the form it took. And while subsequent changes were generally expected no-one anticipated the form they were to take.

Since the demotion of Malenkov, and what appears to be a clear-cut victory of a heavy industry faction in the Praesidium, diplomats here had become bolder in their speculation. The favourite game lately has been to draw up a roster of "Malenkov men" and evaluate their chances of political (and physical) survival....

[Watkins then details several of the other personnel changes in the Kremlin hierarchy.]

The first conclusion to emerge from all these Cabinet shuffles is Malenkov's present isolation. As a mere Deputy-Chairman he now trails, more obviously than before, behind all his former fellow members of the Praesidium and by many observers here he is regarded as a finished man. He appears to be the only member of the "discredited faction," if there was such a faction, to have been punished....

Why Malenkov should have been selected to take the blame for everything is even more mysterious since the promotion of people who were thought to be associated with him in the policies he advocated as head of the Government.

— **March 28, 1955 (Letter 246)** —

[Watkins and Kazakevich spent a day visiting museums in and around Moscow. Their discussions, and the day's events, touch on the universality of youth.]

... When we came out to get into the car, there was the usual crowd of about 50 boys and men standing around staring at it. It is the only Oldsmobile in the Diplomatic Corps and invariably attracts a crowd wherever it waits, for the youngsters especially are quick to notice the different lines and get as close as possible in order to be sure not to miss any of the fascinating details. Often they touch it and sometimes they rest their satchels on the fenders. The old chauffeur, Maxim, who is terrified of getting the paint scratched, says that he thinks he will have to ask the Canadian Government for a bonus to make up for the wear and tear on his nervous system. Kazakevich thought that it was the flag that attracted attention and asked if the city regulations required him to fly it. Maxim said that it was appropriate to fly the flag when the head of mission was in the car but would not admit that he had orders to do so, although no doubt he has. I said that I did not think that it was the flag the boys were interested in and Maxim confirmed this. It was the lines of the car in general, which were different from any other in the corps, and the chrome ornament on the front in particular — a jet plane. Often remarks were made about this: oh, a *reaktivny* [reactionary] plane, they are trying to scare us, etc....

At the time of the First World War, as I knew, the Futurists, poets and painters or would-be poets and painters, had affected various *outré* styles of dress and personal adornment, such as painting a flower on their cheeks. As we could see in Moscow, some of the young people were wearing long hair and zoot suits but in Leningrad recently, Kazakevich had heard, one young man had created quite a sensation by coming to his classes in the University with his nose painted green. It seemed to me that we were coming along rather quickly these days. There had been an orchestral concert a few days ago in the Hall of Columns consisting of works by Benjamin Britten and Carl Nielsen plus Gershwin's *Rhapsody in Blue*. The audience, I had heard, was largely made up of young ladies with short bobs and long-haired young men in zoot suits who made it quite plain during the playing of the Gershwin by lolling their heads and flopping their arms that they were very much in the groove. An all-Wagner programme a few days later was another sign of the times....

People were pretty tired of hardships, Kazakevich said, and the only way of persuading them to accept further sacrifices was to convince them that they were necessary for their own defence. Stalin could have done it without that, but nobody else could. Stalin had said that there must be an enormous increase in steel production, and now the Soviet Union was second only to the United States and ahead of Britain. This position had not been achieved without great sacrifice. Stalin had simply said that the steel must be produced and no nonsense about it; if anybody tried to make trouble or sabotage the effort, shoot him.

But none of the present leaders could get away with that. The people would not accept additional hardships without good reason. If they were required for military reasons, they would understand and accept. That would be normal. Russia had always been a military state, and the rule of a Party, such as they had had since the Revolution, was something new in Russian history and, so to speak, abnormal. But for the army the people would find it natural to make further sacrifices....

Kazakevich said that he did not believe that the Russians, in spite of not being able to travel and see for themselves, believed the stories so frequently printed in the *Literary Gazette* and other papers about American workers being hard up and living poorly. On the contrary, so far as he could see, they probably exaggerated the wealth of the United States and were convinced that the country was full of great warehouses stocked to overflowing with all sorts of commodities that it would be very desirable to have here. What stumped them was how to get hold of the exchange to purchase some of these good things. The example of the United States as a model producing country had been held up to them so constantly and strenuously before the war that it would take more than the Soviet press to convince them of a serious decline. What they did seem to think from what they read, however, was that somehow or other the Americans had gone Fascist since the last war. That seemed to be the only explanation for many of their actions, e.g. travel restrictions, refusal to allow people like Paul Robeson to visit Moscow, etc.

John Watkins.

(*left*) Soviet leader Josef Stalin
in 1952, one year before his
death.

Georgi Malenkov,
Communist Party
Secretary, in 1953.

(*below*) May Day parade,
Moscow, 1947. Kremlin towers
and garden are on the left.

Moscow street in the 1940s.

View from the gate of the Canadian embassy, Moscow, 1949.

Canadian embassy, Moscow, during Watkins' tenure as chargé d'affaires and ambassador.

(below) Entrance to the residential area of the Canadian embassy.

Courtyard, Canadian embassy. Note the vegetable garden and stack of firewood on the left.

Workers' housing, Moscow, 1940s.

ohn Watkins, left, with Canadian External Affairs Minister Lester Pearson, right,
nd Soviet ambassador to Canada Dimitri Chuvakhin in the Crimea, 1955.

Pearson sharing a joke with Communist Party leader Nikita Khrushchev
and Soviet Premier Bulganin in 1955.

On his return from the Crimea, Pearson is interviewed in front of the
Canadian embassy in Moscow by reporter René Lévesque.

Getting to Know
Anatoly and Alyosha,
Spring and Early Summer, 1955

Watkins here recounts a conversation with Professor Anatoly Nikitin, also referred to as "Tolya," who presented himself as an historian from the Moscow Academy of History specializing in American foreign policy. They had met in late December 1954 through Nikitin's purported sister, Nina Krymova, an expert in Scandinavian literature. In a despatch at that time, Watkins described his new acquaintance as about 40 years old, "a short, stoutish man with a round fresh-coloured face, light brown hair,... a prominent forehead, pale grey eyes behind rather thick glasses, a slightly retroussé [turned up] nose, a pleasant smile, and small plump hands."

Nikitin in fact was Anatoly Borisovich Gorsky, a high-ranking KGB officer who also used the cover name Anatoly Gromov. From 1936 until 1944, Gorsky was stationed at the Soviet Embassy in London where he helped direct a handful of moles, including Kim Philby, Guy Burgess and Donald Maclean. He later moved to the United States to direct Maclean in espionage activities against the American government. One-time Soviet spy Elizabeth Bentley knew Gorsky as "Al" when she worked under him in Washington, D.C. She described him as "a short, fattish man in his mid-thirties, with blond hair brushed straight back and glasses that failed to mask a pair of shrewd, cold eyes." He was transferred to the Soviet trade mission in Japan, and in the early 1950s returned to Moscow, where he worked under Oleg Gribanov, a high-ranking KGB officer who masterminded the entrapment against Watkins.

In Moscow, Gorsky used the Professor Nikitin cover as late as the mid-1970s to attempt to deceive foreigners, including Robert Ford, Canada's ambassador to Moscow in the 1960s. Gorsky spoke fluent English with a British accent, and led Watkins to believe he had useful connections in the Kremlin. The RCMP Security Service later concluded that the operation against Watkins was planned from the moment he set foot in Moscow, and that the elaborate ruse is evidence of the importance the KGB placed on winning over a Western ambassador. Watkins, on his way to higher levels in External Affairs, would have been a tremendous prize, far more valuable than a lowly embassy clerk or guard.

If Watkins suspected a KGB connection, he did not report it in the despatches and letters extant. However, about a month after meeting the "professor," he wrote to Ottawa: "I assume that Mr. Nikitin, having worked in the Foreign Ministry, has made sure that it is safe for him to come to the Embassy and that he will probably be questioned about his conversations with me. One must at least act on that basis with all Soviet contacts ...” (Letter 71, January 24, 1955 — not reproduced)

— April 4, 1955 (Letter 277) —

[Watkins and Nikitin attended a theatre offering an evening of comedy cabaret.]

... After the theatre Mr. Nikitin came home with me for a cup of tea. He was away behind in his reading of the foreign press and did not know what was going on in the world. Was there anything new on Formosa [Taiwan]? Not that I knew of. He could not understand the American attitude on that question and could assure me that the average Soviet citizen found it quite inexplicable. If you asked anybody in the street, he would not understand why there should be any doubt that Formosa belonged to China. It seemed to people here that the Americans were taking the same attitude towards the Chinese Revolution that some of the western countries had taken towards the Russian Revolution at the time of the intervention.

Mr. Nikitin had noted that the Soviet press had not had anything recently on the question of a Soviet-Japanese peace treaty and wondered if anything had appeared in the Western press. The last I had seen was that the Soviet and Japanese Governments had agreed on New York for the negotiations. That had been announced in the Soviet press, Mr. Nikitin said, and he supposed that the Japanese had some kind of observer status in the United Nations and that the head of their delegation would be in charge. I thought that the Japanese would probably like to have the southern part of Sakhalin back. Yes, Mr. Nikitin said, and probably the Kurile Islands, too, and maybe even Okinawa!

Mr. Nikitin had read a copy of *Time* I had given him at his request. He would have brought it back but did not like to take it to the theatre. It did contain some interesting facts, he thought, but much of the news was distorted for propaganda purposes. It was here too, I said. Well, he supposed there was some of that everywhere. I gave him some Soviet examples which he could not refute. He wanted to know if the article in *Pravda* for March on American troops in Canada had given the full agency report or had just made appropriate selections. I had not yet seen how the report had appeared in the Western papers. He did not suppose in any case that it was anything very new. It was well known, I replied, that Canada and the United States cooperated on joint defence problems in the North and quite natural that they should do so. He did not question this.

Mr. Nikitin had noticed that the Canadian Minister of Foreign Affairs [Lester Pearson] had stated recently that Canada would not necessarily be involved if the United States got into war with China over the coastal islands. I said that the Minister had made it quite plain in a recent speech that if either Canada or the United States were involved in a war for their very existence it was unthinkable that the other could stay out — even for a couple of years, as the Americans had done in the last two World Wars. On the other hand, we were not automatically involved in any local war in which the United States might be engaged. We hoped, and I was sure also that the Russians hoped, that the Formosa question, for instance, could be settled by negotiations. Mr. Nikitin did not believe that the Chinese could be persuaded to negotiate with representatives of Chiang Kai-Shek.

On the old question of the single-party system here, which there is really not much point in discussing with Russians, Mr. Nikitin said that the whole population was represented by the Communist Party. What group would another party represent? I thought that perhaps the farmers might like to have a party of their own. They already had 40 per cent of the membership of the Supreme Soviet, Mr. Nikitin said. It seemed to me, however, that they had been called upon to make the largest sacrifices for the development of industry and that the reason why the agricultural situation was not better after all these years was that the peasants had felt neglected and had never put much heart into their farming. They had always been opposed to collectivization and as for the *agrogorod* [literally 'farm city'] scheme, they had made it quite plain that they did not want to give up their small cottages to live in hypothetical apartment houses. It was a normal peasant reaction anywhere. They were always passionately attached to the soil and the thought of not owning a bit of land, however small, seemed monstrous to them. I knew many farmers in Canada who could not understand how people could bear to live in an apartment, however luxurious, without any lawn or garden, and who would not dream of leaving the farm when they retired unless they could buy a small house and garden in town. Not long ago I had seen a cartoon in *Krokodil* [Soviet humour magazine] showing all the peasants working hard on their own plots and telling an old *babushka* that she had better go and do some work on the *kolkhoz*.

Admittedly, Mr. Nikitin said, the agricultural situation was bad and it was receiving lots of healthy criticism in the Soviet press. But it would be wrong to draw the conclusion that the Soviet peasants as a whole were dissatisfied with the regime. There had been a kind of agricultural party before — the Social Revolutionary Party — which had identified itself completely with the wealthier farmers and lost all support from the peasantry. There were undoubtedly peasants who would like to own their own farms and who did not cooperate whole-heartedly in the work of the *kolkhozes*, but they were a minority of ''survivals from the past.'' You could hardly expect to change the peasant mentality in a generation, but the young people were aware of the advantages of large-scale farming, as opposed to the uneconomic units of the past. Nobody here would say that it was Utopia or deny that there were many tough problems to be solved, but few would argue that the basis was wrong and that was the main thing. Mr. Nikitin wished that the rest of the world would just leave the Russians alone to solve their problems in their own way.

I said that the rest of the world felt very much the same with regard to the advice of their local Communist parties who advocated a Soviet solution of quite different problems. In a recent *Pravda* article on American-British economic rivalry in Canada, the author had concluded by praising the efforts of the Labour-Progressive Party[1] but had not indicated that it represented about 1.1 per cent of the population. I supposed that Russian readers thought that these Communist parties abroad, about whose activities so much was written in the Soviet press, were large and influential. Mr. Nikitin did not believe that they were under any such illusion, but he could not see why the Soviet press, if it agreed with the views of the Labour-Progressive party in Canada, should not say so.

The following is an account of Watkins' first meeting with Alexei Mikhailovich Gorbunov, or Alyosha, ''a dark-haired, pale faced, well-dressed man of about forty'' as he is described below. Gorbunov was introduced to Watkins as another professor at the Institute of History, and as a consultant to the foreign ministry. In truth, Gorbunov was Oleg Mikhailovich Gribanov, the second-highest ranking official of the KGB's Second Chief Directorate, responsible for intelligence opera-tions within the U.S.S.R. Gribanov was the mastermind of the black-mail operation against Watkins, and the chief actor in the deception.

Within the KGB, Gribanov was known as ''Little Napoleon'' for his ruthless scheming and forceful personality. He was apparently recruited

into the KGB in the early 1950s following a career as a trained Soviet
diplomat. Gribanov was decorated for organizing mass arrests during
the 1956 Hungarian revolt. He is also reported to have planted a mole
inside the British Embassy in Moscow in 1955, a spy who eventually
found a post in Naval Intelligence in Britain. And in 1958, he success-
fully blackmailed the French Ambassador, Maurice Dejean, using a
heterosexual love-trap. This last operation employed the same ruse
tested on Watkins two years earlier, when Gribanov pretended to be
a friend holding the KGB at bay.

Watkins records a suspicion that his new acquaintance had access
to secret police files (see Letter 547, July 20, 1955, reproduced below),
although nowhere in the despatches extant does he state explicitly that
he regards Gorbunov as a KGB agent. In the following account of
their first meeting, Watkins inaccurately refers to Gorbunov as
"Alyasha."

— April 15, 1955 (Letter 317) —

... Mr. Nikitin had also invited two friends, one of whom brought his
wife. He introduced them just by their names and patronymics and I
have forgotten even those. One, whom they called Alyasha, was a
"scientist" of some kind, I think a colleague of Mr. Nikitin's in the
Institute of History, a dark-haired, pale faced, well-dressed man of
about forty. The other, Valadya, was a member of the Institute of
Agriculture and looked rather like a farmer....

There was plenty of good food and drink and most of the conversation
was in a light bantering tone. Much fun was made, for instance, of
Mr. Nikitin's *penchant* for rather snappy bow ties. In Russian, Mme.
Krymova said, they were known as *sobáchy radost* (a dog's joy). I
came to Mr. Nikitin's defence and assured him that he was in good
company, for our Foreign Minister [Lester Pearson] almost always
wore bow ties. "Did you hear that?" Mr. Nikitin shouted, "The Canadian Foreign Minister wears bow ties. Now what have you got to say."
On this point they were discreetly non-committal but they insisted that
the colour combination on Mr. Nikitin's tie was really too-too. I said
that in Canada or the United States it would seem rather conservative.
This amused them hugely and they began to refer to him as "the
Conservative."

Some fun was made of Mr. Nikitin's brief period as a diplomatist. Alyasha, in particular, who looked much more like the magazine diplomat than Mr. Nikitin, was inclined to poke fun at the profession. He could not see why the Soviet Ambassador (what was his name by the way?) and I did not do much more to promote cultural exchanges between our two countries.... How many Canadians had visited the Soviet Union last year? I was not sure of the exact figure but guessed that including Ukrainian-Canadians it might have been close to 100; in any case a good many more Canadians had come here than Soviet citizens to Canada. Well, that was probably because they would not let these terrible Communists in or because nobody invited them. And most of those Ukrainian-Canadians were just tourists visiting relations. Why didn't we have Canadian artists come here to perform? I did not know that any had been invited. And what about an art exhibit? He thought that Mr. [Dimitri] Chuvakhin, [the Soviet Ambassador to Canada] was not doing much. I said that I was afraid our contemporary painters were too formalistic. I had not heard of any exhibits of Western European painting here. I mentioned that a pathologist and a meteorologist had come here for a conference and that several Soviet scientists and Red Cross people had gone to conferences in Canada. But that was just international conferences and did not mean much, he said; Mr. Chuvakhin and I should arrange more cultural exchanges.

Watkins was invited to spend two days in the country with Nina Krymova, her "brother" Anatoly ("Tolya") Nikitin and several of their friends. The gathering took place at the dacha of the senior agriculture official whom Watkins had met at Nikitin's apartment in mid-April, Vladimir Yefimovich Kondratov, or "Volodya." Also joining the group was Alexei "Alyosha" Gorbunov. The trip was a clear attempt to isolate Watkins from associates in Moscow, and to gradually make him feel a part of the group.

— June 7, 1955 (Letter 463) —

...we turned to the right on a country road and soon reached the dacha. [The community of] Bolyshevo ... still has the air of a small Russian village but no doubt the city will soon engulf it too. There are already two or three rest homes for artists and actors in the neighbourhood and quite a few dachas.

Volodya's dacha was not the ordinary log cabin type but a large stuccoed house in the centre of a couple of acres of land with many large trees, lilac bushes, dwarf cherry trees in blossom, flower gardens, and a vegetable garden. The property was surrounded by a high wooden fence and there was a small wooden cottage beside the gates, in which the gardener and handyman and his family lived. Maxim, our chauffeur, asked if he might leave the car there over night and go to his own dacha, which was not far away, and this presented no difficulty. It was left outside a small building which seemed more like a tool shed than a garage. In fact, there was no sign that Volodya had a car of his own, but he probably has the use of an official car and chauffeur.

Volodya and his wife gave us a cordial welcome and had our bags carried in to a large airy bedroom with lots of windows, very plainly furnished with two narrow metal beds, a large old desk, a rug and a couple of chairs. The house had been "remonted" this spring and everything was fresh and clean. The ceilings were high with cornices and the walls were papered in light colours with small patterns unlike the flamboyant wall papers being put on most of the new apartments in Moscow. Tolya and I shared this room. Mme. Krymova and Volodya's wife used the other large bedroom. Volodya slept on a cot in a wide hall off which the bedrooms, bathroom and kitchen opened. The other guest slept on a couch in the glassed-in porch in which we ate our meals. When it is too cold, they use the living room, which was also very plainly furnished but contained a large dining table. The house had no upstairs but there was an attic for storage over part of it. It looked as if it might have been built 60 or 70 years ago.

When I suggested that the house was solidly enough built to live in all year round, Volodya said that that was true but that at present only part of it could be heated. One side of a Russian tiled stove going right up to the high ceiling protruded into the living-room and the other into the bedroom in which I slept. The plumbing was old-fashioned but worked — except for the wood stove for heating the bath water, which gave off plenty of heat but declined to yield any hot water. I am afraid that I caused a good deal of extra work by saying, when asked, that I would like a bath on Sunday morning, for the water had to be heated on the kitchen range and poured into the bathtub.

The back of the property went down to the steep right bank of the Klyasma River (the same in which I had bathed last summer in Vladimir, some five hours from Moscow by train). There was a locked gate in the wooden fence along the river bank but anyone who wanted to go down and take a dip in the Klyasma was welcome to the key. Only

Tolya was hardy enough to go down on Sunday morning and he reported that the water was unpleasantly cold. He pointed out to me a patient fisherman who had been at it since five o'clock and in six hours had caught only one small fish. A few cows and goats were grazing along the bright green banks of the river and groups of young people were lying lazily in the sun. The whole village was delightfully rustic and unspoiled, and although there was running water in Volodya's house, most of the inhabitants obviously got theirs from the well in the centre of the village green.

Alyosha, a colleague of Tolya's in the Institute of History, whom I had also met at his apartment, arrived about ten minutes after us in a big shiny Zim driven by a chauffeur, who came out for him again the next day. He apologized for being late and for appearing in a rather formal-looking dark suit, but he had just come from the office. Half an hour after Alyosha's arrival we sat down to supper. I had brought along some Canadian rye, Danish *akvavit* and French red wine. They had vodka, beer and a dry white Georgian wine. The table was well laden with *zakuskis* [hors-d'oeuvres] — cold ham, sausage of different kinds, sliced cucumbers in sour cream, etc. — a whole meal in themselves but not to Russians. The cold collation was followed by an excellent soup, boeuf strogonov, cake and coffee.

After supper they played Russian dances, tangoes, waltzes, etc. on the victrola and those who felt like it danced. The machine was a large one combined with a radio which did not seem to be in very good order but with which we had had to bear, Mme. Krymova protesting vigorously, until Alyosha, a Torpedo fan, had got the final result of the Czech-Torpedo football game (2-1 in favour of Torpedos).

The moon was full and the nights are never very dark at this time of the year, although not as "white" as in Leningrad. We sat out in the garden for an hour or so and they sang song after song. Alyosha has a good tenor voice, although untrained, and the rest did their best with what they had. Mme. Krymova, who as usual had been working too hard on her Scandinavian translations, went to bed about midnight. The rest of us stayed out in the garden with rugs over our shoulders, for it got rather chilly in spite of the Canadian rye, until about one o'clock.

When I got up at ten on Sunday morning, Tolya had already had his dip in the river but Volodya and Alyosha were still sound asleep. It was therefore well after 11:00 when we sat down to breakfast. The Russians, like the Norwegians, seem to eat the same kind of food for breakfast as they have had for cold supper the evening before — ham, various sausage meats, cucumbers, cheese and even cold fish. For my benefit Mme. Krymova had made toast and I stuck to that with a little ham and tea. The others started with the bottle of French wine which they pronounced excellent.

There was much good humoured banter at the table about the evening before, most of it at the expense of the short, stout Tolya, who was said to have been seen wandering about with bottles hanging around his neck. The three men have been friends at least from their student days, when they were apparently always together and were known as the three musketeers.

After breakfast the conversation turned to more serious subjects. Alyosha wondered how foreign diplomats in Moscow reported to their governments on Soviet conditions and opinions since they did not associate much with Russians. They had to base their reports largely on the press, I replied. But newspaper articles could often be interpreted in different ways and it would surely be useful to discuss them with Russian intellectuals. I agreed that it would be very useful indeed but did not think that the diplomats could be blamed for not doing so, when Russians intellectuals were afraid to have anything to do with them. Had I not made many friends here? I had been exceptionally lucky on my first posting here and had made a few Russian friends with whom I had spent many pleasant hours. There had been no secrecy about it. I had visited them in their apartments and had gone openly in the Embassy car with the flag flying. But they had preferred not to visit me at the Embassy. Since I had come back this time, however, they had done so, but one of them had told me that when he had mentioned doing so to a friend, the man was horrified and said that he would not take 30,000 roubles to venture inside a foreign embassy.

It seemed as if this must be leading up to something and finally the point was reached. Tolya and Alyosha had had a conversation on this subject recently with a mutual friend, Peter, on a very high desk in their Ministry (culture). "Peter-on-the-high-desk," as Tolya called him, had informed them that it had now been agreed at the top that it had been a great mistake to cut the foreign representatives in Moscow off from contacts with the Soviet intelligentsia and that the restrictions had now been removed. (Hitherto they have never admitted that there were restrictions and have made lame excuses to try to hide their embarrassment.) It had also been decided, he had told them, that the officers in the Foreign Ministry should be permitted now to associate with foreign diplomats on a social and unofficial basis.

(There have been signs of this in recent weeks. The head of the section dealing with the Netherlands invited the Ambassador and his wife and one or two other Dutch officers to a luncheon at the new Prague restaurant on Arbat Square, gave them a good meal with excellent Georgian wines, and conducted the whole affair in the most civilized and pleasant way. At a concert in the Bolshoi about a week ago Mme. Teplova, the wife of the former Chargé in Ottawa, asked me in a rather pointed way what the inside of our Embassy was like. I had not too bad a conscience, however, as I had invited her to the July 1 reception last year and she had not come. Her husband had said that she was at their dacha. I said that I supposed she was at the dacha again this summer. She was, she said, but it was not very far from Moscow!)

They had decided also, Tolya said, that it had been wrong to be so ashamed of their inadequacies. There were a great many things that were still not as they should be and, as I knew, they admitted and criticized these things very frankly in their papers, but considering the terrific destruction of the last war, much of which would still take many years to recover from, and considering the terrible hardships the whole population had suffered, they had perhaps not done too badly and need not be over-sensitive about their shortcomings.

Alyosha supposed that some of the diplomats, the Americans, for instance, were very prejudiced against, and critical of, everything in this country. He did not imagine that they would want to have Russian friends. On the contrary, I said, I was sure that many of them would welcome the chance. I supposed that there might be officers with certain prejudices on any staff but American officers I had talked to seemed to be fair and objective and eager to get as accurate a picture of Soviet life as they could. This seemed to cheer him up considerably. (The word ''objective'' is coming into good odour again.) But of course when the atmosphere was poisoned by press attacks and abuse from both sides, I added, it could not but affect the individuals who were doing the reporting. Tolya and Alyosha agreed but said that they thought the atmosphere was improving. Did I think that the U.S. Ambassador [Charles Bohlen] was an *umny chelovyek* [''bright guy'']? Yes, I thought that he was a very intelligent man. Moreover, he spoke Russian well and was well acquainted with Russian literature. They had heard that he spoke Russian fluently.

The Commonwealth seemed to be an enigma to them. What were the relations of the Commonwealth heads of mission in Moscow? Like any others, I said, except that we met together, more or less regularly, every two weeks to discuss matters of common interest. The meetings were more in the nature of friendly chats than anything else. There was certainly no attempt to influence anybody's attitude towards any particular question, if that was what they thought. But there were a number of questions, Alyosha noted, on which India and Pakistan did not agree. Such subjects, I said, were not discussed. As they knew, the Commonwealth Prime Ministers occasionally met to discuss Commonwealth and world affairs. They often had a very frank and useful exchange of views and in the course of the discussions some of them might very well change their views as a result of the information or reasoning of others but there was no attempt to force anybody's views on anybody else. That would defeat the whole idea. On some subjects they simply agreed to differ. (I have never had much success in explaining the Commonwealth to Russians and I cannot say that Alyosha looked much enlightened, but perhaps if he reflects on the new Soviet attitude towards Yugoslavia, it may put him on the right track.)

Volodya wanted to know how much our chauffeur was paid. We have to pay so much more for all servants than Russians do that I think he was surprised. He then wanted to know how much I was paid. (Russians have no inhibitions about asking or answering such questions.) Unfortunately I had to admit that I did not know exactly and he probably thought I was either stupid or secretive, but I told him approximately and was relieved to find on checking that it was not too far out.[2] I also explained the allowance system and rubbed in the ridiculousness of the official rate of the rouble.

On the subject of cars, Alyosha said that the Soviet makes were too old-fashioned in appearance to sell well abroad but that the new Volga should do better. He had seen one and it was much smarter looking than the Pobeda or the Zim with lots of glass all around the back like some of the American cars. I asked him how he liked his Zim. It was a pretty good car, he replied, but a little weak in the back end. The Pobeda was the sturdiest and by far the best for country roads but it was not very handsome.

At two o'clock we had chicken with rice and more tea and at three we left for Moscow. Alyosha was also going home early as he had a lecture to prepare for the next day. I invited them all for dinner at the Embassy the next Saturday evening and they accepted with alacrity. Alyosha said that he hoped I would visit him at his dacha near Yalta this summer. Tolya goes down every year and was planning to fly about July 1. I said that I had long been planning a trip to the Crimea and could probably get away for ten days about July 5. I had thought

of driving. Volodya said that it would be much more interesting to
drive than to fly and that it would be useful to have the car while there.
I asked Tolya if he would not like to drive with me instead of flying?
He thought this might be managed. Nina had taken her vacation in
May, owing to her husband's illness, and would not be able to get
away again. Besides she had to go to Helsinki as translatress for the
Soviet peace delegation around the end of June. Vera, Volodya's wife,
was very anxious to go, but Volodya, who expected to be too busy
with his *kukuruza* (maize) at that time to take a holiday, was not sure
that he would trust Vera in such company. After the way Tolya had
acted last night he would have to think it over. Further discussion was
postponed until Saturday evening when we would all meet at my place.

— June 30, 1955 (Letter 491) —

[Watkins met Anatoly Nikitin and Alyosha Gorbunov for dinner at a small restaurant
near the Canadian Embassy. The conversation quickly turned to the evening the pair
had spent two weeks previous as dinner guests at the Embassy.]

… Since the evening at the Embassy Alyosha had been worrying because
they had stayed so late and made so much noise. He was afraid that
they might have embarrassed me and that someone on my staff might
report to Ottawa that I had been entertaining Russians. I said that on
the contrary if the others had not been otherwise engaged I would have
asked them to join us and they would have been happy to meet more
Russians. But could anyone on the staff write to Ottawa and report
that I was entertaining Russians? They certainly could if they wanted
to, I said, but it was no secret from the Department that I had made
a few Russian friends during my first posting in Moscow and a few
more this time. Why should it be? We would all welcome the chance
to get to know more Soviet intellectuals. Alyosha was glad to hear
that I had not been embarrassed by their staying so late and having
such a good time. I hoped that they would come again....

As an extension of criticism and self-criticism, I suppose, an order has
obviously gone out recently to Soviet officials to ask foreigners what
they do not like or take objection to in the Soviet Union. I had this
question from a young army officer in a restaurant in Gorki Park about
a week ago. Other foreigners have had the same question from Foreign
Ministry officials and others. Last night, Alyosha put it to me, prefac-
ing it with some remarks about how conscious they were of their many

inadequacies and how eager they were to correct them.

I said that of course one thing that struck all foreign visitors to Moscow was the crowding and the lack of housing space — not that there was not a housing shortage at present in many countries, but it seemed to be particularly acute in Moscow. This they were well aware of, Alyosha replied, and as I could see from the tremendous amount of building going on in Moscow they were trying their best to meet the situation. When he had been in Vienna with the Soviet delegation, he had seen most of the city and many of the suburbs and had been surprised that there had been so little new building since the war. The bombed spots had been neatly cleared but were still unbuilt. And they had been working on the restoration of the Opera for ten years and still had not finished. People in the West had little idea of the tremendous destruction the war had caused in very large areas of the Soviet Union and how much rebuilding had been done and was still to do. But at least anybody could see that they were working hard and trying to provide more housing space as quickly as possible.

I felt like saying something about the shoddiness of much of the new building but thought perhaps I had better save that for another time. As an example of a minor irritation which could easily be corrected, I referred to the habit of sending out invitations to concerts or receptions only a day or so, and sometimes only a few hours, in advance. I had had an experience of it just that day. Anatoly had telephoned on Monday to make sure I would be free for dinner on Tuesday at 8:00 and I had said that I would. There was a Swiss reception at 6:30 but that left plenty of time. Then on Tuesday afternoon an invitation had come from the Ministry of Culture to a concert [that night]....

Anatoly said that it was a good idea to air any complaints I had to Alyosha because he could take them right to the top....

I said that on the whole I found life in Moscow very pleasant and did not wish to complain, but since they asked, there was one thing that I thought should be considered and that was the very high official rate of the rouble. It meant that everything purchased here was fantastically expensive when translated into foreign currencies at the official rate and for foreign representatives living here their governments had to compensate either in the form of very large living allowances or, as in our case, of a subsidized rouble....

The Czechoslovak coup of 1948 came up in conversation with a discussion of post-war tensions. In my opinion it marked a divide. Up to that point the Soviet Union had had a great deal of good will, largely in gratitude for the exploits of the Red Army and partly, in Scandinavia, for instance, for the promptness with which the Soviet Union had withdrawn from places like North Norway and Bornholm. The Czechoslovak coup had made many countries fear that their own Communist parties would try something similar. Anatoly said that as I knew the Czech Communist Party had had over forty per cent of the vote in the last election and it had been an internal matter. He did not know why everybody blamed the Soviet Union for it when there had been no Soviet troops in Czechoslovakia. There were plenty of troops round about, I said, and nobody had any doubt that it was Soviet influence that turned the trick. I wondered how the people in jail in Czechoslovakia and other places for Titoism were feeling now that Titoism had become respectable — not to speak of those who had been shot for it. Alyosha said that it was not for Titoism that those people had been punished but for treachery; they were accepting dollars to betray their country; why, one of them had had two villas in Switzerland!

The U.S. intelligence, he said, continued to carry on diversionary activities wherever it could. Had I not heard that they had sent over a thousand diversionists into China? It was well known that for China's industrialization steel was the most important industry. There had been two big explosions in the big new steel plant being built at Ashon. This was the work of the Americans who were trying as hard as they could to prevent China from industrializing. I had no information on this subject.

There was some discussion of the Soviet press and Anatoly and Alyosha argued that there was no demand here for the kind of yellow journalism that flourished in the West and no reason that they could see for allowing it in any case. I said that it seemed to me that there could be more foreign news in the Soviet papers and that some of the long articles they published in their four-page papers used up too much space. Alyosha said that for himself as for most of the Soviet public it was extremely interesting to read progress reports in agriculture, building, etc. from various parts of the country and also criticisms of enterprises in which things were not going as well as they should. Probably most of this domestic material was very dull reading for foreigners but it meant a lot to Soviet readers. The papers could perhaps be expanded to include more foreign news but as I knew they were short of paper. They could not begin to meet the demand for books.

I said that they certainly often published very large editions. In spite of that, he said, people were starving for more books.

Alyosha was very strong on the point that the Soviet Union did not interfere in the internal affairs of other countries. Nobody could say that the Soviet Union was advising any communist party anywhere to try to overthrow their government. The Comintern, of course, had done so but it had been disbanded. Anatoly had heard that communist papers like *Humanité* in France made themselves ridiculous by pretending that everything in the Soviet Union was perfect whereas Soviet papers were constantly criticizing all sorts of defects. Alyosha thought that this was stupid but said that of course the Soviet Union could not interfere with how other Communist Parties ran their papers!

A Visit to the Crimea,

July 5 to July 14, 1955

Watkins and several of his new Soviet acquaintances took a trip July 5-14 to the Crimea where they stayed at the well-appointed dacha of Alyosha Gorbunov and his wife. It is likely Gorbunov's dacha, along with his "wife," were borrowed for the occasion through the resources of the KGB. Watkins later reported on the entire trip (see next despatch), but first sent this letter to Ottawa because it recorded "the only serious conversation I had with my host ... in the four days I spent at this dacha." In it, Watkins revealed that Alyosha's contacts in the Kremlin were more extensive than he realized initially.

— July 20, 1955 (Letter 547) —

... Alyosha, who is Anatoly's superior in the Institute of History of the Academy of Science and a consultant to the Ministry of Foreign Affairs ... must be a pretty senior official. This was the immediate conclusion of a young Soviet assistant to the Minister of Highways whose acquaintance we made on the road to Yalta and whom Alyosha kindly invited to dinner. He had no idea who Alyosha was and I could tell him only that he was a member of the Institute of History but he said that it was obvious that he was a big shot from the size of the dacha and garden, from the big Zim and chauffeur (actually Alyosha had two chauffeurs at his disposal) etc. He must certainly hold a high executive position, the young man said. Did he have an apartment or a house in Moscow? I did not know but supposed that he had an apartment. (I have since learned that he also has another dacha not far from Moscow.)

Alyosha made it plain that he had close contact with Mr. Molotov but also with Messrs. Bulganin and Khrushchev. They had both, he said, mentioned to him that they were sorry not to have been able to be present at our July 1 reception. They had been busy on a very important matter and would have had to come half an hour later than the others, which would have been *nyeudobno* (inconvenient). I said that of course I would have been very happy if they had come but that I had been surprised when so many as five members of the Government had arrived. Alyosha asked if we had ever had so many at a Canadian reception before and I said not so far as I knew. Anatoly, who had come to the reception, had also made this point and the implication was, I take it, that Alyosha had strongly recommended attendance, although he did not come himself and may indeed have been working at the time with Messrs. Bulganin and Khrushchev on the "very important matter" on which they were engaged....

Alyosha, who was born in a farming village in the Urals, does not speak English or, so far as I know, any other foreign language, but he may be able to read English. At least he is well read in the Western press and knows a great deal that is not printed in the Soviet press. In fact, I cannot remember having referred to any news item concerning international affairs with which he was not already familiar. It is possible that he is supplied daily with very extensive summaries in Russian translation from the British, American, French, German and Swiss papers. Perhaps, Anatoly, who knows English extremely well, is one of his sources....

With reference to the travel situation, Alyosha noted that only a few border regions were now closed to foreigners and remarked that even these restrictions might soon be removed. If only the Americans could be a little less zealous in their intelligence activities, he said, the problem would be simpler. I doubtless knew that a number of Americans had been sent out as *persona non grata*. I did and I knew also that a number of Russians had been sent home from Sweden and other countries for similar activities. But it was not only the U.S. Attachés who were engaged in this business here, he said; all the young diplomatic officers were also working for the intelligence service wherever they travelled. Did I know that all the younger U.S. and British officers were forbidden to associate with Russians? I thought he must be mistaken. I knew, for instance, that some of the British officers who spoke Russian well seemed to have many Russian acquaintances. I had often seen them talking to them at receptions. That was just at receptions, he said. He knew for a fact that they had orders not to associate with Russians; and that was too bad, because they would leave here after a couple of years without really getting to know any Russians....

Alyosha said that he was hoping to see me occasionally at his home in Moscow when he and his family returned from their leave. If I did not mind dining with them alone, he thought that we could occasionally have more serious discussions of international problems than in a larger and more frivolous group. Even if the picture now seemed a little brighter, there were still many problems to solve and he thought that we could have mutually profitable discussions. He said that he knew Mr. Molotov thought highly of my judgment. I expressed surprise since I had never talked to Mr. Molotov for more than ten minutes in my life.

Alyosha had emphasized again the point he had made a few weeks ago that a great responsibility rested on the foreign representatives and that what they observed and reported undoubtedly influenced the attitude of their Governments towards the countries from which they were reporting. It was therefore very important they they should have the chance of discussing affairs in the country in which they were posted with members of the intelligentsia who could help to interpret the press and explain the policies being followed.

Alyosha seemed not only to know the Diplomatic Corps in Moscow rather well but also the foreign journalists, what agencies or papers they represented, who was whose assistant, how they acted at receptions, who had the most brass, etc. How much of his knowledge comes from gossip picked up by Foreign Ministry officials at receptions and how much from secret reports of the M.V.D. [i.e., the KGB] it is of course impossible to know, but my guess would be that he has access to information from both sources.

— July 28, 1955 (Letter 558) —

On Tuesday, July 5, at 2:00 PM I called for Mme. Krymova's brother, Mr. Anatoly Nikitin, at his apartment on Pushkin Street to start on our long drive to the Crimea, where we had been invited to spend a few days as the guests of his friends Mr. and Mrs. Alexei Mikailovich Gorbunov (Alyosha and Anya) in their summer dacha at Alushta, about 45 kilometers from Yalta. We had decided to take it easy on the way down and spend the first night at Oryol, the second at Kharkov, the third at Zelyonny Gai (Green Hill) arriving at the dacha on Friday, July 8. It is about 1500 kilometres from Moscow to Yalta.

... The road was excellent all the way, with the exception of some detours on account of road repairs between Moscow and Tula, and it was possible to drive at a steady 65 or 70 miles an hour for long stretches. Except near large cities and towns, the traffic was not very heavy, although many Russian families in Zims and Pobedas were taking the same sort of holiday and the hotels at Yalta and Alushta and probably many other coastal towns were full to overflowing. I do not suppose that the regime has even begun to understand yet how much Soviet life and society are bound to change as more and more of the population acquire automobiles.

We had taken some lunch with us — not very much because it was sure to spoil in the hot car — and picnicked near Tula the first day and near Kursk the second. After that what remained had to be thrown away and we got lunch for the third day from the hotel in Kharkov. I had wired ahead for reservations and three comfortable rooms were waiting for us in the old-fashioned hotel at Oryol when we arrived at about 9:00 PM. There was even a bath with my room and with Anatoly's but Tuesday was not a hot-water day, they told us. There is evidently a shortage of electric power in Oryol, for the street lighting was very dim. So we had a cold bath that evening and a warm one next morning.

Just before reaching Oryol we had driven into a showy new *zapravochnaya stanzia* (gas station) elaborately fitted up with red gasoline pumps, garages for storing cars, workshops for repairing them, etc. The architecture for these wayside gas stations was too bastard for precise definition. It certainly was not Russian. Anatoly thought that the high square ornamental towers with their steep red tile roofs suggested South German origin. They are probably intended to stand out from the landscape and that they do as effectively and gaudily as most of ours. In fact, I was beginning to feel quite at home in this peculiarly gas-station ambience until we discovered that in spite of all the trappings they had no gas — a characteristically if not exclusively Soviet feature.

Maxim reported some difficulty in getting gas the next morning in Oryol and Anatoly took over. He got the secretary of the City Soviet on the phone and explaining the situation in my name in much better Russian than I could have done soon extracted a promise of immediate attention to our needs. In all fairness, however, it should be admitted that this was the only time on the whole trip that there was any difficulty or delay. Otherwise we were always able to fill up with the best quality gas in 15 minutes, although we had had reports from the British and others that it was frequently a 2-hour operation....

After we had been on the road a couple of hours the next day, the engine began sputtering and Maxim Constantinovich decided that the gas he had got in Oryol had not been of high enough quality and that it would be better to add some from one of the cans in the back. Also the accelerator pedal had come off and needed to be screwed on again. We decided to have lunch under a tree by the roadside sitting on the rich carpet of grass, clover, and many kinds of wild flowers. Maxim soon discovered that in the rush of getting ready (he had just returned from leave) he had forgotten to bring either a screw driver or a piece of hose. So he began to ''vote,'' as he expressed it, and waved his hand in the air at every car and truck that passed. Most of the drivers paid no attention and the two or three who stopped could not help. Finally a shiny new green Pobeda with sheer pale-green curtains pulled up, an exceptionally tall, slender, smartly dressed young lady got out, and Maxim announced in jubilant tones that at last he had found a "good soul" who was willing to help him.

[The car was fixed with the help of the young lady, Natasha, and her cousin Boris, both of them travelling to the Crimea for a holiday. Watkins and Anatoly then continued on to Kharkov.]

... I had spent almost a week at the Intourist Hotel in Kharkov in the fall of 1950 and had been very comfortable there. The same old Intourist official was on the job and gave me a warm welcome. In the meantime he had acquired an assistant, a nice-looking young Ukrainian woman who spoke a little English and was very polite and helpful. I was delighted to find also the same waiter I had had five years ago. He shook hands and cordially welcomed me back to Kharkov. As before the food was excellent — much the best we had on the trip — and the service perfect. The waiter, now over 50, was trained in the old school and knows his job. We had caviar with toast and butter, steaks done exactly as we ordered them, salad, and strawberry ice-cream. Anatoly talked about Natasha all through dinner and as we walked through the city for an hour before going to bed. He also kept asking at the desk if she had registered, although this was complicated by the circumstance that he did not know her surname.

Kharkov was a sad sight when I first saw it in 1950. It had changed hands several times during the war and been bombed by both sides and although many new buildings had been constructed, there were still whole streets of empty shells. It looks infinitely more cheerful now. There has been a tremendous amount of reconstruction, including of course many grandiose official and institutional buildings. Streets have been widened and much space formerly built on has been used for squares and gardens and the banks of the rivers have been or are being turned into parks. The population was given as 833,000 in 1938 and is probably well over a million now....

A large crowd had collected around the Oldsmobile while it was waiting in front of the Intourist Hotel. It attracted some attention everywhere we stopped but not more than in Moscow: it is the only Oldsmobile in the Diplomatic Corps and all the youngsters are very curious and ask many questions. Maxim is very short with them and objects to having it touched with ice-creamy hands. To his disgust Anatoly remembered after getting into the car that he had left his passport under his pillow. When he went back to get it, the hotel manager said that it was lucky he had not got away because a telephone call from Moscow had just come in. It was the head of his Institute, Professor Sidorov. A request had just been received from a Kharkov youth group for a lecture on current events and since Anatoly was in Kharkov anyway perhaps he would give the lecture and save sending somebody from Moscow. Anatoly replied firmly that he was on vacation and would most emphatically not give any lectures on anything for a solid month. Professor Sidorov was greatly disappointed....

[In the meantime, Natasha and her cousin Boris caught up again with Watkins and Anatoly. The pair had been shaken but not injured by a motor accident.]

Natasha's spirits had been much restored by a good Kharkov steak for breakfast, and it had been agreed that we should have a picnic lunch somewhere along the road and that they should be our guests for dinner at Zelyonny Gai in the evening. Anatoly and I stopped for a dip in the Oryel River, (Anatoly pointed to the prevalence of bathing suits at the various swimming holes in the region as a sign of advancing culture.) As we finished, the green car pulled up beside ours and we agreed to lunch at the first shade trees we found. Large trees were scarce in this region. There was nothing but the steppes, like a sea of grain, for miles and we had to drive almost 100 kilometres before we found a small grove on the edge of a little village consisting entirely of small white-washed thatch-roofed cottages. Anatoly persuaded the housewife in the nearest cottage to boil some water for us so that we could use our Nescafe. Although the cottage was small and had a rather tumble-down look from the outside, Anatoly said that it was clean and tidy inside. At first the woman had feared that it would take some time to get the water boiled because she had let the fire go out, but Anatoly spotted a primus stove in a corner and they used that. Boris bought a jar of butter-milk from an old man who lived alone in another cottage. His cow was tethered on the roadside in front of the house and his little mongrel dog was keeping watch. As in all these little villages, there were chickens and geese wandering along the side of the road. All the men and girls were away at work on the *Kolkhoz* haying or harvesting.

At a small town called Novomoskovsk we all visited a large and beautiful old wooden church, which stood out against the horizon for miles with its cluster of nine onion-shaped cupolas of different sizes and heights. It had been built 300 years ago by the Zaporozhye Cossacks, the priest who was just preparing for a service told us and not a nail had been used in its construction. It had been struck by a shell during the last war but had not been seriously damaged, as a stone or brick church would have been by a similar blow. The shell had simply come in through one wall and gone out through another. The interior was beautifully finished, entirely in wood, the work of highly skilled crafts-men. The priest showed us their oldest ikons, including a beautiful 12th century one from Byzantium, and drew our attention to a beautiful enamel cross bordered with large diamonds which he was wearing. We were told that the handsome new Zim standing in the courtyard belonged to him. The congregation was just assembling — mostly old and middle aged peasant women with a few men and children. One old woman informed us that we should not hold our hands behind our backs in a church, but we had no idea why.

Zelyonny Gai, where we were to spend the night, was nothing but a large gas station with a hotel and a couple of restaurants, garages, work-shops, etc. The rooms were spacious, clean and comfortable but without baths or even wash basins. When we asked for a bath, they said that there was no hot water but when Anatoly complained, they agreed to light the wood stove at the end of the large bath tub and produce some. Although the hotel, with its ornamental square tower and red tile roof, was only a few years old, it was disintegrating quickly. Tiles had fallen off the roof and not been replaced and there were water stains on the ceilings. The plumbing was of poor quality, the locks were hard to work, and the door knobs had disappeared from some of the doors.

We had dinner in a pleasant open-air restaurant but the food was not very good. The chef came in for a consultation and said that the only meat course he could recommend was a Hungarian goulash which was at least edible. Fresh tomatoes, cucumbers and strawberries with ice cream made up for the other deficiencies. Anatoly and Boris tried the *okrashka* (cold Kvass soup mixed with sour cream, a summer deli-cacy which I abominate) but could not eat it. Natasha drank some French wine that I had brought with me; the rest of us a harsh Ukrainian Vodka and mineral water.

A good deal of landscaping had been done around the gas station and although the trees had not yet grown very high there were many pleasant walks through the flower gardens. There was also an orchard of cherry, apple and pear trees and at a reasonable distance from the hotel a cow stable, pig sty and hen house. It was the kind of clear, silent moonlight night one reads of in Gogol and after dinner Anatoly and Natasha wandered off to a secluded arbour in the garden. My role was clearly indicated and as I walked [Boris] around the property I found out a little more about him....

The next morning Anatoly and I started off on the last lap of our journey. Natasha's car had to stay for a while in the garage at Zelyonny Gai but it was plain that we would be seeing her again in Yalta. I shall have to leave my account of our visit at Alyosha's dacha until next week.

— July 30, 1955 (Letter 585) —

Not far from where the main highway turns south to Simferopol, Alyosha met us in his handsome black seven-passenger Zim (an adaptation of the Buick).... I was seated in the front seat beside the chauffeur, Zhora; Anatoly and Alyosha sat in the back. Both front and back seats were covered with bright new rugs of good quality and very comfortable to sit on in that hot climate. Maxim was told to follow, and Zhora, who is familiar with the tortuous roads of this mountainous region, drove as fast as he could all the way....

It took us about an hour and a half to reach Alushta. Our hostess, Anya, a medical doctor, was out at the gate to meet us. The dacha was a well-built stucco house of four rooms set in the midst of a luxuriant garden of about an acre and a half. There were apple, pear, apricot, peach, cherry and even fig trees, grape-vines, strawberries, raspberries, black currants, and all sorts of vegetables. A small mountain stream ran diagonally through the garden and insured a plentiful supply of water. The gardener, Ivan Ilyich, had had the brilliant idea of putting in a large concrete basin about five feet wide, ten feet long and six feet deep and it made a very pleasant little swimming hole. A large towel was hung up as a curtain on the house side, and the trees and shrubs made it more or less safe on the other three sides. There was a bench to sit on and not far away a couch for taking sun baths.

We had all our meals at a table under a large apricot tree just outside the glassed-in verandah. Beside it was a large comfortable swinging divan, well-equipped with bright-coloured cushions, and just around the corner of the house, a hammock. Part of the cooking was done in a small inside kitchen (it contained a large electric refrigerator and a trap door leading to the wine cellar) and part in a tumble-down cookhouse about twenty yards from the house. Ivan Ilyich's wife did the cooking. There was no upstairs in the house but a room had been built for Ivan Ilyich and his wife on top of the house at the back. It was reached by an outside stairway and from the landing there was a good view of the Black Sea.

After a refreshing dip in the cold water of the basin, we had our first meal. It started at about eight o'clock in the evening and went on until after midnight. Alyosha had long been promising that when we arrived he would hoist the admiral's flag and we had wondered what he meant by it. It turned out to be a cocktail which he claims to have invented consisting of cognac, rosé muscatel and Riesling — for the admiral's flag was tricoloured. It was very smooth and palatable but had a kick like an elephant. One was enough for me but Anatoly, who ventured a second in addition to sundry other beverages, had to be helped to bed shortly after midnight. Alyosha, who also had two, was not affected at all. Anya drank only Riesling.

My bedroom, at the front of the house, was large and airy. The whole place seemed to have been done over recently and was spotlessly clean. (This was only the third summer that Alyosha and his wife had had the dacha, although they had had another one in the Crimea before that; it probably came along with a promotion.) A door at one end of the bedroom opened into a small sun-parlour. The bathroom was just across the hall. It had a toilet and a large old bathtub but no basin. The hot water tap was not running but Ivan Ilyich heated water for me every morning and carried it in pails from the cookhouse....

... Alyosha arranged for a motor-boat, a "cutter," as they call it, to take us by sea [to Yalta] — about 40 miles. On the way we visited an "artek" — an exclusive summer camp for children from eight to fourteen, formerly used for the children of soldiers killed in the Civil War and later for Spanish refugee children. It is beautifully situated right on the sea shore and attractively laid out with flower gardens, shrubberies and shaded walks. A young woman from the first-aid building showed us around and treated us to mineral water in the large open-air dining-room — it had a roof but no walls. A hundred or more children were having dinner. They were well tanned and looked healthy and happy. The food was plain but abundant and the children were well-behaved. Anatoly asked if any of them spoke English, and two girls, aged nine and thirteen, were brought over. They were too shy to say much but seemed to understand quite well what we said to them, especially the younger, a thin little girl with pigtails and large round spectacles. There was instruction for the children in carpentry, arts and crafts, sewing, etc....

[Watkins and Anatoly had a drink at a Yalta hotel on arrival.]

Alyosha had asked me to try to get Anatoly home by four o'clock ... Yalta was terribly hot and the trip back on the cutter was very refreshing....

The next morning at about 11:00 we set off in two jeeps to visit a large forest preserve or *zapovednik*. Anya had long been wanting to see it but Alyosha had always found some good excuse for not going. After we had been on the road in the jeep for a while, I understood why. I was in the front seat with the driver and had to hang on for dear life or be bounced out on to the road-side. There was a bar across the road at the entrance to the preserve, which was lifted only after the woman in charge had carefully examined Alyosha's permit. She had a neat little house just inside the gate, and a swarm of children suggested that she did not lack male company, although no husband was in evidence. Alyosha had to present his permit again to get out of the preserve some 50 kilometers away from where he had entered. No hunting is permitted but a few years ago the herds of deer had got so large that they were doing damage on the neighbouring *kolkhozes* and a brief open season had been declared.

We had a picnic lunch at a beautiful spot which had formerly been the site of a monastery. A student from Kharkov University, who was working there for the summer, told us that a group of ecclesiastical dignitaries had recently visited the sacred spring (from which we all had a drink of good cold water). The liveliest member of the group had been an 87-year-old nun....

On the hill-top where we had lunch there was a small house occupied by an old forester and his wife. The last Czar had had a summer palace not far away and used to come there to hunt, he told me. When I asked if he had ever seen Nicholas II, he said that he had talked to him just as he was talking to me. "Now you have a Czar, and now you don't," he said, "and what can you do about it?" He and his wife had four children but they all lived in the city. For his part he never went into town; he preferred to go to the woods. People who were not used to it would not be able to live there the year round as he did. They would go mad from loneliness. But he had been born not far from there and had spent all his life in the mountains. His wife said that it was often very cold in winter, and this year they had had a frost on May 20

which had spoiled the cherry and apple harvest and had made it necessary to set out new tomato plants. They had two cows and a few pigs
and chickens and a large garden and orchard....

Late in the afternoon we drove on to Yalta, through more and more
miles of beautiful forest and over equally bumpy roads. We were guests
of Anatoly for dinner at a fashionable new Yalta restaurant built on
the side of a mountain with a beautiful view of the city and the harbour.
We were all too tired to take much interest in food, however, and the
young people dancing to a jazz orchestra had no competition from our
table. Alyosha had had his chauffeur bring the Zim into Yalta to drive
us home and we got back to the dacha at about 2 AM....

[The following day Watkins and the others spent a quiet day reading, bathing and
talking while Anatoly visited Yalta again.]

The next morning Anatoly, for whom Alyosha and Anya had waited
up until after midnight, telephoned from Yalta to suggest that we drive
over, pick him and his friends up, and visit the winery at Massandra
nearby. This was an interesting excursion. Massandra is the oldest
winery in the Crimea and has a famous "library" of wines from all
over the world. The oldest bottle we saw was a sherry from 1775.
They had hidden the library when the Germans came and had poured
all their own wine out into the streets. The inevitable degustation was
something of an ordeal, not that there were not some very good wines,
but many of them were sweet and strong and the amiable director
preferred to see us drink bottoms up.

I was sick as usual ... but recovered sufficiently to eat some lunch.
Anatoly ... had to be helped upstairs and treated with valerian drops
for his heart. He slept it off in about an hour and we drove back to
the dacha to celebrate Anya's birthday.... We had a quiet pleasant
evening and the next morning at nine I left for Moscow.

We were surprised to see so many gypsy caravans on the road south
of Kharkov. On the way back we must have seen about 200. They
were travelling in crude four-wheeled carts, drawn by two or more
horses, with spring colts running alongside, and heaped high with rolls
of quilts and swarms of children. Some of the old bearded patriarchs
looked handsome and dignified. I would like to have stopped at one
of their encampments and talked to some of them but we were deter-

mined to get back to Moscow in two days — and did. Maxim informed me that the Soviet authorities had tried to organize the gypsies into the system and make them work but had finally had to give it up as a bad job. It was just like trying to make the Jews farm in Birobidjan, he said; it could not be done. They spent all their time trading and driving hard bargains with each other and did no farming to speak of. He had heard that in Israel they were good fruit farmers but that was different. The gypsies, he said, lived mainly by stealing, although of course they made a pretense of mending pots and pans. There had always been large numbers of them in the Ukraine because the country was rich and the people were generous. In his region, Tver, there had been a few but people had disliked and feared them and would not give them much. I asked if they were not now required to send their children to school. It was not possible to make them do so, he said, because they were always on the move.

A Visit by the Minister for External Affairs,

Summer and Autumn, 1955

Two Canadian cabinet ministers visited the Soviet Union in 1955, James Sinclair (1908-1984), the Minister of Fisheries, and Lester Pearson (1897-1972), then Secretary of State for External Affairs. Sinclair (whose daughter Margaret was later to marry Prime Minister Pierre Trudeau) attended the seventh session of the International Whaling Commission in Moscow on July 18, and wrangled a visit to some fishing stations in Siberia. The area was off-limits to virtually all Westerners, but two political considerations caused the Soviets to make an exception of the rather insistent Canadian fisheries minister. First, Sinclair said he intended to call on the new Chinese revolutionary government in Peking following the Siberia trip, but would not if the Soviets denied him a look at the fisheries. The Kremlin did not want to forfeit a chance to encourage closer Red Chinese-Canadian relations, since it could help pry Ottawa out of the American orbit. Second, Pearson was to visit the Soviet Union in October (see below) and the Kremlin was determined to make it a success. Refusing Sinclair access to Siberia, as Watkins argues, might have soured Pearson's visit before it began.

As it turned out, Sinclair's trip was an almost comic disaster. Two days after the following despatch was written, Sinclair broke his left leg and damaged his spine during a visit to Petropavlovsk, a coastal community on the Kamchatka Peninsula. As he was taking a photograph of the harbour from a catwalk, the scaffolding collapsed, and the fisheries minister fell about 20 feet to the ground while beams, boards and seven associates landed on top. Sinclair was laid up in hospital for about a month, and to add insult to injury, was prevented from returning directly home afterward. The Soviets insisted Sinclair carry on with his visit to Peking, despite persistent pains in his leg and back.

Pearson's visit had its own comic touches, many of which are retold in his memoirs. The trip came about after the Soviet Foreign Minister, Viacheslav Molotov, cornered Pearson during ceremonies in San Francisco marking the tenth anniversary of the signing of the United Nations' Charter on June 26, 1945. Molotov extended an invitation for an autumn visit to Moscow, without offering any special reason. Pearson was the outstanding Western diplomat of the period, someone the Soviets likely felt they could trust to convey to NATO members their new willingness to normalize relations. He was also someone they believed would discuss the aims of the Western alliance more freely than his

NATO colleagues. For the external affairs minister, it was an opportunity to assess personally the post-Stalin regime and perhaps pin down just who was in charge at the Kremlin. After consulting with Prime Minister Louis St. Laurent, Pearson accepted Molotov's invitation and built the visit into a twelve-country, six-week world tour. The Soviet leg was from Oct. 5 to Oct. 12. Preceding it was a trip to Ottawa by Watkins during which he briefed Pearson and made final arrangements for the visit.

A handful of officials from the Department of External Affairs accompanied Pearson, including George Ignatieff, the head of the defence liaison division, and John Holmes, formerly chargé d'affaires at the Moscow embassy. Both were fluent in Russian, and Ignatieff, whose father had been education minister under Czar Nicholas II, was born in St. Petersburg (now Leningrad). Also in the group was Associate Deputy Trade Minister, Mitchell Sharp, who later became trade minister, then finance minister under Pearson, and external affairs minister under Trudeau. Sharp's task was to hammer out a trade deal with the Soviets, and he did arrange a big wheat sale (see introduction) that was signed several months after Pearson's visit.

The highlight of the trip was a drinking contest on Oct. 11 at the Crimean dacha of Khrushchev, with Bulganin present. The evening began on a feisty note as Khrushchev and Pearson jousted over the true purpose of NATO, all recorded by a CBC Radio reporter with politics in his own future, René Levesque. In his recently published Memoirs, *Levesque describes Pearson as "on the canvas" at the end of the exchange, although Pearson's memoirs call it a draw. The audio tape was late in being broadcast in Canada because, according to Levesque, External Affairs had put a temporary embargo on it for fear it would embarrass the minister during his world tour. The future Quebec premier was outraged: "It was enough to make one ... separatist!"*

No reporters were present during the most raucous part of the evening when Pearson, Ignatieff, Watkins and another External Affairs official, Raymond Crépault, sat down to a feast with their Soviet hosts. Many shots of vodka enlivened the conversation, and as Pearson proudly records: "About 12:30 the four Canadians marched straightly, heads up, with fixed determination and without any assistance, to our car, after a very spirited leave-taking. We left our two Russian hosts in worse condition than we were...."

There is a persistent story that during the evening, Khrushchev mocked Watkins for his homosexuality by declaring during a toast that not all those at the table loved women. This account originated in the mid-sixties with a defecting KGB officer, who was not present but had heard the story from fellow officers. However, there are compelling reasons to doubt its authenticity. Pearson's memoirs do refer to Watkins' declining spirits during the evening, but this was likely due to over-indulgence; Watkins, who would soon develop diabetes, could not take large amounts of alcohol without feeling ill. Ignatieff, whose Russian was more fluent than Watkins', insists in his own memoirs and affirmed in an interview that the incident did not take place. As the only surviving member of the four Canadian guests that night, his recollection stands as the last word on the subject in the absence of fresh evidence to the contrary.

While the diplomats and statesmen tested their livers, Levesque, also fortified by liquor, decided to take a skinny dip in the Black Sea. He writes: "It was almost the end of me. The water was treacherously mild for a full stomach, and a very strong current carried me out beyond the promontory behind which the villa was hidden. Seeing that I was being transported into a vast bay that stretched to the horizon, I made a supreme effort and managed to struggle back until finally a wave threw me up on a rock, nearly skinning me alive."

Watkins' despatches are necessarily thin for the trip as Pearson's aides recorded most of the day-to-day discussions. Fortunately, he did report his impressions of the drinking session, giving us a third written account (after Pearson's and Ignatieff's) about that extraordinary night. There is no reference to the infamous (and likely apocryphal) Khrushchev toast.

The trade agreement, the first of many wheat deals to be signed with the Soviet Union, was an important achievement of the trip. The visit also confirmed for the West that Khrushchev was in charge, something Ignatieff conveyed in writing to NATO leaders immediately after Pearson departed the Soviet Union. But Canadian-Soviet relations on the whole remained unchanged. On the latter part of his world tour, Pearson made some provocative remarks about Soviet inflexibility in foreign affairs that drew the wrath of Kremlin officials. The crushing of the 1956 revolt in Hungary, as well, dissipated any remnants of goodwill the visit may have fostered.

For Watkins, the trip broadened his relationship with Alyosha Gorbunov, since many of its details — including the sidetrip to the Crimea — were arranged through the mysterious professor of history.

The despatches presented in this section were written both before and after Pearson's visit. They have been arranged here to track the course of that visit.

— August 2, 1955 (Letter 569) —

[Watkins met Anatoly Nikitin and Alyosha Gorbunov for dinner at the latter's apartment in Moscow.]

... While Anatoly was there, most of the conversation was about our visit to the Crimea and his various escapades. Alyosha said that he had had to go to Simferopol for a couple of days and during that time Anatoly had simply disappeared....

... [Alyosha] wanted to know whether our Minister of Fisheries, Mr. Sinclair, had enjoyed his visit to Moscow and had been pleased with his reception ... I said that Mr. Sinclair had enjoyed his visit ... and was very much pleased that arrangements had been made for him to see the Pacific coast fisheries.

Alyosha said that obviously a Canadian Cabinet Minister had not come to Moscow merely for the Whaling Conference. He no doubt had other reasons both for coming here and for returning home by way of Pekin[g]. Mr. Sinclair had mentioned, I said, that the Prime Minister had thought his visit a good idea and considered that it would be useful for one of his Ministers to have first-hand knowledge of the Soviet Union. Alyosha suggested that it would depend somewhat on Mr. Sinclair's impressions whether Mr. Pearson would come in October. I said that so far as I knew Mr. Sinclair's attendance at the Whaling Conference had been planned months ago and had no connection with Mr. Pearson's visit, which had been decided upon after Mr. Molotov had invited him in San Francisco. In fact, Mr. Sinclair might decide to visit other countries before returning home and might not be back in Ottawa for several weeks. Mr. Pearson had already announced in the House [on July 11] that unless some unforeseen emergency arose he expected to visit Moscow early in October ....

(No doubt many Soviet officials have been racking their brains to figure out some connection between Mr. Sinclair's visit and Mr. Pearson's. This would only be typically Russian. And I suspect that it is largely on this account that Mr. Sinclair got his trip to see the Pacific coast fisheries. At least he had the impression at first that they were trying to fob him off with a visit to the Black Sea and Caspian fisheries instead and made it plain that as a British Columbian his main interest was in the Pacific fisheries. If he could not see those, he proposed to return to Canada via Leningrad without visiting any fisheries and to tell people at home that there was no use coming here because you could not see what you wanted to see anyway.)

It is plain that Mr. Sinclair's plan to travel through China had also intrigued the Russians. Alyosha wondered if this meant that Canada would soon recognize China. I said that it was well known that we had been close to recognizing China shortly after the British had done so but I had no information about any such intentions at present. In Alyosha's opinion the visit of a Cabinet Minister, even unofficially, could not be without significance. He noted that the French Prime Minister and Foreign Minister had recently spoken about the possibility of establishing relations with China but had not yet made any official moves. Perhaps their remarks were trial balloons to test U.S. reactions.

At least Mr. Sinclair must have been convinced by his visit here, he said, that the Russian people did not want war and had no intention of attacking anybody. What had he found to criticize? The rouble rate, I replied at once. He had translated all prices into dollars at the official rate and had been horrified to find that an ice cream cone cost over 50 cents, an orange 75 cents or a dollar, an ordinary meal $10, etc. When we had asked if he was going to take home any souvenirs for his small daughters, he replied most emphatically not at such fantastic prices.

Alyosha thought that Mr. Pearson's visit in October should result in better and closer relations between Canada and the Soviet Union. I said that Mr. Pearson would obviously not be coming with any intention of pulling us further apart. After all, as Mr. Sinclair had mentioned ..., we were neighbours in the Far North. Alyosha thought that Mr. Pearson's visit should do a great deal to improve relations....

[Alyosha] had seen that our Prime Minister had said that a Soviet parliamentary delegation would be welcome in Canada and that the question of a Canadian delegation could be considered after Mr. Pearson's visit; also that Mr. [Prime Minister Louis] St. Laurent had felt that an invitation to Mr. Bulganin should come first from the United States. Alyosha looked as if he thought that a somewhat remote possibility but said that no doubt Mr. Molotov would be invited to visit

Canada some time after Mr. Pearson's visit here. He also referred to
the exchange of American and Soviet agricultural delegations and the
forthcoming visit of the latter to Canada [from August 25 to September
10, a trip chaperoned by Watkins]....

— August 18, 1955 (Despatch 616) —

["You" in the following despatch refers to Lester Pearson.]

Over the coffee-cups in his discreetly lighted study ... Alyosha said
that there were a few matters he would like to discuss with me with
regard to your forthcoming visit to Moscow. Did I know, for instance,
of any particular questions you would wish to raise while you were
here? I mentioned that the question of an exchange of parliamentary
delegations had come up in the House not long ago and that it had
been suggested that a decision might be made after your Moscow visit.
Otherwise I had no information about any particular questions that you
would wish to discuss but I might have after I had talked with you in
Ottawa in September.

Alyosha said that the Soviet Government regarded your visit here
as extremely important and sincerely hoped that it would result in
improved relations and closer connections between Canada and the
Soviet Union as well as contributing much to the relaxation of international tension in general. Since it was after all an official visit of
the Canadian Foreign Minister, it was clear that both would wish to
discuss practical problems and produce concrete results which would
benefit both countries. I said that although I had not yet had a chance
to discuss the visit with you it was obvious, as I had remarked before,
that you had accepted Mr. Molotov's invitation in the hope that your
visit would result in better relations and I was sure that the Prime
Minister, the Cabinet, and the Canadian people shared that hope.

Alyosha said that he had been asked by somebody high in authority
to let me know in confidence before my departure for Ottawa several
topics which the Soviet Government would wish to raise so that you
could be prepared to discuss them and perhaps take concrete action on
some of them. They all had to do with the matter of improving relations
between our two countries and helping to relax international tension.
So as not to overlook anything, he had jotted down a few notes. He
took a small piece of paper out of his pocket....

[Watkins here lists the six areas of concern raised by Alyosha, including cultural and scientific exchanges, and a general trade agreement.]

When I noted that no date had yet been fixed for your visit and that ... there were certain difficulties about a date in October because both Mr. Molotov and Mr. Bulganin had gone on leave and were not expected back in time, Alyosha said categorically that Molotov would be back by October 1 and so would Bulganin....

The Soviet Government was anxious above all that you should really enjoy your visit to the Soviet Union. I said that I hoped and fully expected that Mrs. Pearson would accompany you. That would be doubly delightful, Alyosha said, and they would depend on me to let them know what would interest you most and would do their best to plan accordingly....

I said that I had been wondering whether you and Mrs. Pearson would stay at the Embassy ... Alyosha said that a private house ... could also be arranged for you if you would like it. A dacha could also be put at your disposal. Or you could be put up in a hotel. Or, if you preferred, you could stay at the Embassy. It was for you to decide.

— October 14, 1955 (Despatch 728) —

[Again, "you" in the following refers to Pearson.]

On Monday afternoon, October 10, at 3:30 PM, as you will remember, I went with you to call on Mr. Kaftanov, the First Deputy Minister of Culture. With him, in addition to the Soviet Ambassador in Ottawa, Mr. [Dimitri] Chuvakhin, and the translator, Mr. Pavlov, were two senior deputies of the Ministry of Culture....

The most signal characteristic of the meeting was the alacrity with which the Russians agreed to all the exchanges proposed. On matters which did not come under the Minister of Culture, Mr. Kaftanov promised that they would be brought to the attention of the authorities concerned and expressed assurance that they would be interested.

The exchange of scientists and technicians, for instance, Mr. Kaftanov said, was now under the Ministry of Higher Education, which he was sure would be agreeable. The exchange of scientific and technical literature, however, was still under Mr. Kaftanov's Ministry. This kind of exchange was not only possible but highly desirable and in his opinion would be mutually profitable.

Mr. Kaftanov did not seem to have the slightest hesitation in endorsing the suggestion for exchange of information on cultural, ethnological, historical, and scientific work in the Arctic regions.... mentioned

especially [was] the work which has been done in the Institute in Leningrad on the production of grammars and the development of means of
writing the various Arctic languages....

When you mentioned that the exchange in meteorological information, which had been happy and constructive in spite of political
relations, could, perhaps, as you suggested to Mr. Molotov, be further
improved and developed in a better political atmosphere, for instance,
in the field of ice and flood forecasting, Mr. Kaftanov replied that he
considered this very important. It was outside the scope of his Ministry
but he would refer the matter to the appropriate officials and the exchange
could be arranged in the usual way. To Mr. Chuvakhin's suggestion
that some kind of convention might eventually be drawn up to cover
this matter, you agreed that when there had been time to study the
basis of such an exchange, it might be possible to embody the results
in a document of some sort.

Mr. Kaftanov agreed that sports exchanges of various kinds would
be desirable. These matters were handled by the Physical Culture and
Sports Committee of the Council of Ministers. He could not foresee
any difficulty, however, for as was well known, the Soviet Union sent
its athletes to all countries which invited them. Mr. Kaftanov displayed
some knowledge of Canadian prowess not only in hockey but in rowing,
swimming and other sports. Hockey, they knew from their own experience, was also good training for football players and they had many
who were good in both games. In reply to your remarks about the
roughness of hockey, some of the officials referred to similar problems
in football and agreed that sometimes both games were not as "cultured"
as they might be....

When you remarked in conclusion that you had found the discussion
interesting and useful and hoped that it would lay the basis and lead,
now that contacts had been established — contacts which could be
widened in Ottawa — to real developments, Mr. Kaftanov replied that
all your wishes coincided with theirs and that all desired the mutual
strengthening of relations between our countries.

— November 5, 1955 (Letter 801) —

I had thought of sending you [the Department of External Affairs] a
few trivia from the Minister's visit to the Soviet Union to which his
distinguished advisers would hardly have descended, at least in their
cabled reports. But first I was ill, then the Massey-Harris people came

from Canada and U Nu from Burma and now the November 7th festivities and the Norwegian Prime Minister and Minister of Trade are upon us. So I fear that as a result of hypertrophied Soviet hospitality these fond footnotes to history will never get written.

The only conversation on which I took notes was the one which Mr. Pearson had with Mr. Kaftanov, Deputy Minister of Culture, and his associates. I reported on it in Despatch No. 728 of October 14 [see previous]. At the meeting with Messrs. Bulganin and Khrushchev in the Crimea, Messrs. Ignatieff and Crépault took copious notes and there is little that I can add to the account of the conversation recorded in your telegram ... of October 27. All I can do is report a few impressions.

Our preparation for the Crimean visit was not ideal. It came at the end of a strenuous week and of a particularly heavy day. We had had to get up at 5:30 AM in order to fly to Stalingrad in a Soviet plane from the Central Airport at 7:30. To the Minister's acute embarrassment the Diplomatic Corps was lined up on the field at that undiplomatic hour for a farewell-to-Moscow ceremony. Mr. Molotov was there himself, of course, with Mr. and Mrs. [Valerian] Zorin [Deputy Minister of Foreign Affairs] and many officials from the Foreign Ministry, the Ministers of Foreign Trade, Forestry, Fisheries, Heavy Machinery, etc. and a good many M.V.D. types. Needless to say, the Soviet press, radio and television and the foreign press were well represented.

After several hours of sight-seeing and a large lunch given by the Mayor in Stalingrad, a three-hour flight to Sevastopol ... and a long, circuitous motor trip over the mountains and through the Baidaratskaya Vorota, we arrived at the guest-house at Miskhor at about 7:00 PM. This gave us just time for a bath and a change before proceeding up the hill to Mr. Khrushchev's villa at 8:00.

Mr. Khrushchev, who had been informed by Alyosha that Mr. Pearson would like to give him our view of NATO, immediately took the offensive by inquiring why we did not get out of it. The brief exchange of diametrically opposed views on NATO, well laced with persiflage from both sides, which followed, was recorded by our CBC correspondent [René Levesque], who played it over to sundry Moscow journalists and is doubtless now complacently presenting it to Canadian listeners.

Mr. Khrushchev then led the way to a kind of conference room, carefully pointing out all the bathrooms en route, whether in anticipation of the results of his subsequent assault on our digestions or simply as a house-proud ex-plumber eager to exhibit the wonders of

his ex-Yussupov mansion,[1] I do not know. Mr. Pearson and Mr.
Khrushchev sat down opposite each other with the translator, Mr. Troyanovsky, sitting at the end of the table between them. Mr. Bulganin
sat next to Mr. Khrushchev with Mr. Chuvakhin on his right. I sat
next to Mr. Pearson with Messrs. Ignatieff, Crépault and Gorbunov
on my left. (Why Alyosha sat on our side of the table, I do not know.)

Mr. Khrushchev did most of the talking on the Russian side, although
Mr. Bulganin did not hesitate to put in a word when he felt like it.
Several times Mr. Khrushchev interrupted the translation of Mr. Pearson's remarks when he could have spared himself some emotion and
us some oratory by hearing them through, but he habitually interrupts
other speakers, even when they are proposing toasts at dinner, if he
thinks of something funny or in fact if he thinks of anything at all that
he wants to say. He did not seem to relish it quite so much when Mr.
Pearson interrupted the translation of some of his remarks but I did.

Although Mr. Troyanovsky almost always returned to his notes after
these interruptions, stating politely that he had not quite finished translating Mr. Pearson's remarks, and would now like, with Mr. Khrushchev's permission, to do so, there was at least one occasion (and perhaps
Mr. Ignatieff's or Mr. Crépault's notes would show others) when,
owing to Mr. Khrushchev's excitement, part of what Mr. Pearson had
said remained untranslated.

Mr. Troyanovsky is a very able translator in both directions, although
it is, of course, easier for him to translate from English into Russian
than from Russian into English. He told me that he made notes in a
kind of shorthand of his own devising in English for the English speaker
and in Russian for the Russian speaker and then translated partly from
his notes and partly from memory. Interruptions do not make his task
any easier but on the whole he coped very well with them. Occasionally
he softened remarks from one side or the other, sometimes by his choice
of words in the language into which he was translating but more often
merely by his tone of voice. He does not have to be told that a joke
is a joke in either language and almost invariably manages to convey
the spirit, even when an exact equivalent, for idioms, proverbs, and
the like, is difficult if not impossible to find....

It was about 10:00 PM when we were invited to go into the dining
room. The long table was loaded with food in the usual Russian style.
Mr. Khrushchev said that we would ignore protocol and just sit
anywhere; but placed Mr. Pearson on his left with Mr. Troyanovsky
next to translate. After we had been sitting down for a few minutes,

he said that his wife and daughter had been waiting for dinner and asked whether we would mind if he brought them in and we dined *en famille*. After what seemed long enough for something of a search, he came back with just his wife, whom he introduced to all of us. His daughter, he said, had got tired waiting and gone to a movie.

Mme. Khrushchova, a short, plain, gray-haired woman, probably not much younger than her husband, seemed by contrast very quiet, modest and refined. She sat down at the table on my left (I was on Mr. Bulganin's left opposite Mr. Pearson) and between the numerous toasts (she drank only wine) talked pleasantly about the beauties of the Crimea, the Moscow opera and ballet, etc. Mr. Bulganin was very polite and attentive to her in an easy informal way. He frequently clinked glasses with her, called her by name and patronymic, and was obviously anxious to make her feel that she was not being left out of anything in such preponderantly male and increasingly stimulated company.

Mme. Khrushchova greatly regretted that Mrs. Pearson had not been well enough to undertake the Crimean trip as she had been looking forward to meeting her. Mme. Khrushchova also has some remarkable grandchildren. I understood her to say that she had three married daughters and a son. One son was killed in the war.

Mr. Bulganin and Mr. Khrushchev were both particular to emphasize what old and close friends they were. Their friendship dated, Mr. Khrushchev said, from 1923. They were close in their thinking and in constant and intimate touch with each other in their work. This was certainly the impression created by their attitude to each other at the table. Whereas Mr. Bulganin always called Mme. Khrushchova by her name and patronymic, with Mr. Khrushchev he often dropped the patronymic and called him just plain "Nikita." It has been speculated in the Western press ... that there might be increasingly acute rivalry for power between Khrushchev as the head of the Communist Party and Bulganin as head of the Government, but if the evidence of genuine regard and affection for each other manifested at the dinner was simulated, they must both be consummate actors.

Mr. Ignatieff will have told you of the fun Mr. Khrushchev had with his title. He began by asking what relation George was to the late General and went on to say that he had met him through his old Ukrainian friend, the dramatist Korneichuk and had seen a good deal of him in the last few years. Apparently he had found him pleasant and amusing company and had a high regard for his literary ability.[2] He also knew that George's father had been Minister of Education but had to be corrected on the dates. At one point he apologized for calling George "Tovarish" [friend] Ignatieff when he should probably have called him "Graf" [Count] or "vache siatelstvo" [my lord], a jest over which he chuckled for quite some time.

Toasts were proposed in rapid succession and *pertsovka* (pepper-vodka) was preferred to the ordinary brand. Both Mr. Bulganin and Mr. Khrushchev were particularly concerned that Mr. Ignatieff and Mr. Crépault should not get away with pouring their drinks on the floor or filling their glasses with mineral water instead of vodka (a practice for which Mr. Bulganin was recently taken to task at a Kremlin reception.) Alyosha, who has an unlimited capacity for alcohol and seems impervious to the effects, was doing his best to help them. When I had to start skipping toasts, I explained to Mr. Bulganin that I would definitely prefer that the Minister did not have to leave me under the table, he released me from the obligation by saying "nye nado, nye nado [it's not necessary]." It should have been earlier, however, for I had to retire to one of Mr. Khrushchev's many bathrooms. Alyosha, who knows quite well the effect of alcohol on my stomach, came out to make sure that I was all right.

As far as I could see, Messrs. Khrushchev and Bulganin would have been quite happy to carry on, in spite of the presence of Mme. Khrush-chova, until we were all under the table. It would certainly not be the first time either for our host or for Mr. Bulganin. But it was midnight and most decidedly, we felt, after our long and eventful day, time to retire. After an affectionate farewell, a little too Russian in style for the Canadian taste, we wove down the long corridor to our waiting Zises [cars]. I am glad to be able to report that none of us had to be carried upstairs at the guest-house, although certainly my preoccupations for the next quarter of an hour are better left undescribed. How the other members of the party put in the time, I have no idea, except that Mr. Ignatieff, *mirabile dictu*, did not forget his promised telephone call to Mr. [Robert] Dunn [the Canadian press attaché] in Moscow.

None of us could do justice to the Russian breakfast of caviar, smoked salmon, cold ham, hot fish, beefsteak, etc., proffered to us the next morning at 9. At 10 we had to start on the four hour motor trip on the tortuous mountain road through Yalta, Alyushta, and Simferopol to the airport at Saki. I was sea-sick all the way and have no recollection of what was said in the car, if anything. At one point we got out and walked along the road for a few yards. That helped a little but not much.

The C-5 [aircraft] was waiting for us at Saki but Mrs. Pearson and the other passengers had all driven to Evpatoria for lunch and were a bit late getting back. They had had a smooth fast flight from Moscow and were obviously in much better shape than some of the rest of us. The C-4 looked very comfortable and I would have been quite happy to park on one of its sofas but there was still more Soviet hospitality in store for me, of which I have given an account in letter No. 741 of October 17 [which follows].

— October 17, 1955 (Letter 741) —

The Zis in which Messrs. Chuvakhin, Ivanov and Lopukin, my friend Alyosha (Alexei Mikhailovich Gorbunov) and I were to drive back from the Saki airport to Miskhor stopped at the edge of the airfield and waited until the C-5 warmed up in a leisurely way and finally took off for Basra. There was an unexpressed anxiety that something might go wrong at the last moment, necessitating still further improvisations, but as Mr. Chuvakhin noted hopefully, the propellors of all four engines seemed to be cleaving the sunlight healthily in the distance and in a few moments the big plane was in the air and heading eastward.

There was very little conversation in the car on the four hour drive back through Simferopol, Alushta and Yalta to Miskhor. Mr. Chuvakhin slept most of the way. Alyosha, sitting in the front seat beside the driver, only turned round occasionally to inquire how I was holding out in the battle against sea-sickness on the same nasty curved road we had covered with the Minister in the morning. He and Mr. Ivanov got off at one point to send a telegram giving the time of the Minister's arrival at Basra but when I wanted to pay for it he said that he would prefer to be paid in cognac.

It was after seven and already getting dark when we got back to the guest house at Miskhor. The five of us had dinner together at eight but in spite of Alyosha's special tri-coloured cocktail, "the Admiral's flag," (Reisling, rosé muscat and cognac) which I was in no condition even to taste, the conversation was not very animated. After a couple of "flags" the two younger men felt in need of air and went out on the verandah. Alyosha followed leaving Mr. Chuvakhin and me alone. We agreed that the visit had been a great success and that we should try in our respective posts to do all that we could to foster the friendly feelings which had been engendered and to encourage the exchanges in the cultural, scientific and technical fields referred to in the communiqué. At about 10:30 everybody went to bed.

Alyosha said that before we were up that morning he had been up the hill to see Messrs. Bulganin and Khrushchev. It was plain, he said, that they had liked Mr. Pearson and enjoyed their conversation with him. I said that Mr. Pearson had hoped that he had not seemed too argumentative. Not at all, Alyosha said. After his conversation with me in Moscow in which I had said that Mr. Pearson wanted to give them our view of NATO and would like to have a frank conversation, he had conveyed this information to Messrs. Bulganin and Khrushchev who, as he had warned me, were not diplomats and liked plain-speaking. He hoped that Mr. Pearson had not felt that they were too blunt. I thought that Mr. Pearson had been very happy that they had spoken so frankly.

I was afraid that Mme. Khrushchova might have thought that we had all had a little too much to drink. Not at all. She had been very pleased to see that everybody was in good humour and had herself enjoyed the opportunity of meeting the Minister and the Canadians with him. (At least none of us had had to be carried out!)

Mr. Crépault had seemed rather a mysterious figure to Alyosha and Mr. Chuvakhin and since [R.C.M.P.] Corporal [Frank] Brien had not been included in the Crimea trip they were pretty well persuaded that he must be the real R.C.M.P. member of our party. Mr. Chuvakhin observed that none of the officers he knew in the Department seemed to know Mr. Crépault very well. I laughed and said that although I had met Mr. Crépault quite a long time ago, we had not been in Ottawa at the same time. When I was in Ottawa, he had been in New York. Recently he had done a tour in Indo-China. But he was just like any other officer in the Department. They looked doubtful, although Chuvakhin should really know better by this time....

For breakfast the next morning, in addition to fruit, yogurt, cold meats and cheese, they served hot fish and potatoes, hot veal patties and macaroni, and hot cheese-cake in a sour milk sauce, all of which I avoided in anticipation of another long drive over Crimean curves to Simferopol. The pleasant-faced maid looked hurt and said that it seemed to her that Canadians had very poor appetites. (She must have been comforted by the amount Chuvakhin ate.) I explained that we were not used to a heavy meal in the morning but that we all felt that she had looked after us very well indeed. She wanted to know if I would not write something in the book and I wrote that Mr. Pearson had asked me to thank the director and his staff for their great kindness and hospitality etc. She hoped that we would all return soon and stay longer.

The plane which had taken us to Stalingrad and Sevastopol was waiting at Simferopol. I spent all the time on the plane lying on a sofa to recover from the sea-sickness induced by the drive. The others all played dominoes. We reached the Central Airport of Moscow at 4:30 PM and Alyosha's chauffeur drove me home.

Alyosha said that he thought that the fact that we had been able to discuss certain details of the trip together on a friendly and confidential basis had contributed to its success. It sometimes seemed a rather devious mode of operation but I can see now that with the curious mentality of these people it was probably quite useful. They were trying as well as they knew how to give the Canadians a good time and were grateful for any hints about what kind of entertainment might please them etc. Alyosha was always enquiring about the Minister's "mood" and was delighted that he responded so warmly to their efforts to arrange for him to see the things that he had mentioned that he would like to see. It was obvious that he had enjoyed the foot-ball game [Red Army vs. the Torpedoes] (I'm sure his every reaction was reported in the highest quarters) and Alyosha was only sorry that the teams had not been more evenly matched.

Had I seen the presents, he asked, and how had Mr. and Mrs. Pearson liked them? [They included an oil painting, a double-barrelled shotgun, a fur jacket and an oriental rug.] The presents were beautiful, I thought, and Mr. and Mrs. Pearson were delighted with them but at the same time somewhat embarrassed by their munificence. That was just an old Russian custom, he said. The main thing was that they should like them....

— November 17, 1955 (Letter 810) —

[Watkins, Alyosha, and Anatoly were dinner guests at the Moscow apartment of the agriculture official, Volodya, one night. Part of the evening turned into a post mortem of the Pearson visit. Watkins also adds his private speculation about why Alyosha behaved in such an odd manner throughout the Pearson visit.]

... Alyosha is continuing with his English lessons but all that he could be persuaded to say was: "Go to Khall!" which we did not think he had learned from his teacher. At the table he asked if I had seen an account of Mr. Pearson's recent speech in New Delhi. I had not. It was more understanding of the Soviet Union than the speeches he had sometimes made before his visit, Alyosha thought, and he had also spoken about taking another look at the Chinese question. He had referred to the Soviet Union and Canada being neighbours on the north and had said that Canada had a good neighbour to the south but did not always agree with its policies.

In preparation for the Minister's visit Alyosha seemed to have read all the speeches Mr. Pearson had made for several years. Some of them, he said, were very unfriendly to the Soviet Union....

We sometimes assume, I think, that the Russians are much surer of themselves than they are. In the Crimea last summer, as I reported to you, Alyosha said that he would like to exchange ideas with me occasionally on international affairs, in fact had been authorized to do so if I were willing, and felt sure that such conversations would be mutually helpful. I agreed but have to admit that I have been very much on guard and more than a little suspicious. During the Minister's visit he called up from time to time and once I went with him to Anatoly's apartment and once he came here after making sure that I was alone. Before I went to Canada, he had said that he would like to meet Mr. Pearson and would come to the Embassy some time when he had a few moments to spare. Later he decided that he did not want to do that but thought that he would have a chance to meet him, as he did, in the Crimea. One thing that was plain was that Khrushchev and Bulganin did not wish to say that they would like to meet Mr. Pearson until they were sure that he would not refuse. Oriental face-saving, I suppose. In this matter the contact with Alyosha was useful because I was able to assure him at once that Mr. Pearson would very much appreciate the opportunity of exchanging views with Messrs. Bulganin and Khrushchev, if he could do so without interfering too much with their holiday plans. That was all Alyosha wanted and he immediately began to outline the plan which we later followed....

His reason for not wishing to meet Mr. Pearson here in advance, I suspect, was that he was afraid if they talked about international affairs, for instance, Mr. Pearson might quote him in his conversation with the leaders, which might be embarrassing. He even suggested that if he met Mr. Pearson here I need not mention his name. I said that it would be difficult to introduce him without a name. Perhaps he could use another name. That would also be awkward, I said, as I had already mentioned his name to Mr. Pearson and told him about my very pleasant visit to his dacha in the Crimea. In any case Alyosha took no chances on being quoted from Moscow. What he called himself, when he met Messrs. Ignatieff and Crépault, I do not know.[3]

Now that it is all over, I have not been able to think of anything he did that was not directed towards making the visit as pleasant and successful as possible. Certainly it was useful to have had well in advance the points which the Soviet authorities wished to discuss and the forewarning about a communiqué. The evening I went with him to Anatoly's apartment, in addition to inquiring whether we were really interested in a trade agreement or not, he asked how we would feel about including the Five Principles in the communiqué and I said that, while we had no objection to the sentiments embodied in them, we would definitely not wish to refer to them as such in the communiqué, with the result that their inclusion was never formally proposed....

— February 3, 1956 (Letter 82) —

Last night I had supper at Alyosha's apartment with him and Anatoly. It was arranged when they were here for supper on January 27 that we should have a bachelor meal, Alyosha considering that his wife's absence in Leningrad, where she is taking a post-graduate medical course, puts him in that category....

Most of the conversation this time was about international affairs. On January 27 ... there had been a brief mention of Mr. Pearson's remarks about the Soviet leaders' visit to India, which seemed to have annoyed Alyosha. I said that I had been travelling and had not seen even a press account. Mr. Pearson had accused the Soviet leaders of hypocrisy, Anatoly said. Alyosha could not understand how after the frank talk he had had with Messrs. Bulganin and Khrushchev in the Crimea, Mr. Pearson could accuse them of hypocrisy. It must surely have been clear to him that they sincerely desired peace.

... Alyosha asked if I had seen in the morning papers that my Foreign Minister had again been making unpleasant remarks about the Soviet Union....

Alyosha was obviously upset and said in an outraged tone that Mr. Pearson had accused the Soviet Union of having aggressive aims in its foreign policy and of imperialism. He had tried to frighten the Canadian people by telling them that the Soviet Union would attack them across the North Pole. Surely he must have seen when he was here how eager the Soviet people were for peace after what they had come through and that the Soviet Government had not the slightest intention of attacking anybody. I recalled that Mr. Pearson had remarked several times since his visit to the Soviet Union that he did not believe that this country desired war. That was true, Anatoly said. He had said many good things but why should he spoil them by accusing the Soviet Government in an important speech broadcast to millions of people from the Canadian Parliament of aggressiveness and imperialism. And the American papers, Alyosha interrupted, have come out with big headlines to say that the Canadian Foreign Minister, who has just returned from a visit to the Soviet Union, says that the Soviet government plans to attack Canada.

Surely he had not said that. Well, that was the implication; he had said that it was a threat to Canada. And it looked very much, he continued, as if these attacks had been timed to coincide with the arrival in Canada of the Soviet Trade Delegation, since they had appeared in the press on the very day of their arrival and seemed calculated, for some reason, to make their task as difficult as possible. I was sure that this was pure coincidence and that there was no desire to create difficulties for the Soviet Trade Delegation. Anatoly agreed that probably there was no such intention in the timing but thought that the effect must be the same.

But why should he accuse the Soviet Union of having aggressive aims and of imperialism? You could call it what you liked, I replied, but the fact was that the Soviet Union was a kind of large and powerful imperium which, by reason of its power and policy, dominated a large region even outside its own borders. Now I know you are going to come back to your favourite subject, [the 1948 Soviet-backed Communist takeover in] Czechoslovakia, Anatoly put in. Well, there are plenty of others, I laughed, for example, Poland, Hungary, Roumania, Bulgaria, Albania, etc. But these countries had independent governments, Anatoly said. And surely I would not say that the Ukraine, for instance, was a colony in the old 19th century imperialistic sense. I certainly could not agree that the Ukraine was very independent in its foreign policy, for instance, or for that matter any of the others from any evidence I had of their voting in international assemblies, for instance. It was clear that they would not dare vote against the Soviet Union.

Alyosha then took the old familiar line that the reason they voted with the Soviet Union was because they agreed with its policy. There were a great many of these old stock arguments brought forth during the evening and they are certainly not worth reporting.

Alyosha asked if I remembered that during the conversation in the Crimea Mr. Khrushchev had complained about the nasty things said about the Soviet Union in Canada and that Mr. Pearson had replied that he would not say nasty things any more. I could not recall this. You are a good Ambassador not to remember inconvenient promises of your Foreign Minister, Alyosha said. He assumed that Mr. Pearson must have been criticized in the press, both Canadian and American, for having come to the Soviet Union and talked with the Soviet leaders at all. I said that I did not suppose that Mr. Khrushchev had expected

to convert Mr. Pearson to Soviet views on many subjects any more
than Mr. Pearson had expected to turn Mr. Khrushchev into an ardent
supporter of NATO; they had certainly been frank enough with each
other and I thought that that was all to the good. Alyosha agreed, but
said that it was one thing to talk across a table in private and another
to attack the Soviet Union before a large audience....

Alyosha said that the Soviet Government would soon be sending a note
to the United States Government to protest against the sending of
balloons equipped with photographic apparatus over the territory of
the Soviet Union. They had now quite a collection, which they had
managed to bring down. The balloons were equipped with apparatus
weighing about half a ton, including special cameras which operated
automatically and carried enough film to photograph about 4000 kilometers of Soviet territory. It must be admitted that they took very good
pictures, showing roads, railroads, buildings, houses, etc. quite clearly.
They were being launched from various countries around the perimeter
of the Soviet Union, e.g. Greece, Turkey, Sweden, Finland and were
constructed to fly very high on currents in the upper atmosphere which
should carry them to Alaska. They were equipped with signal devices
which come into operation when they fell on land or in the Pacific
Ocean so that they could be found and picked up.

Alyosha was only telling me this because they would soon be sending
a note about it. I asked how they knew they were American. Fortunately
they were quite clearly marked, he said, so that there would be no
question about their identity if the case were brought before the United
Nations, for instance. Were they going to take it to the U.N.? I asked.
He did not know. They might. They had not yet decided. But why
should the Americans want to send such balloons over Soviet territory?
he asked. Why should they want to photograph the Soviet Union so
intensively? What would the Americans think if the Soviet Union were
to retaliate in kind by sending balloons to photograph United States
territory? He was sure that there would be panic in the United States
if they did. But of course they had no intention of doing so. I noted
that it was still open to them to accept President Eisenhower's offer
and photograph all they wanted to in the United States. He did not
comment.

Alyosha was pleased with Mr. Pearson's remarks about China and
asked if we were soon going to recognize. I said that it was well known
that we had been close to recognizing some time ago and that when
public opinion in Canada was in favor of recognition we would no

doubt recognize. When that would be, however, I had no idea. Alyosha thought that it must be clear to everybody now that Chiang Kai-Shek had no hope of taking over the mainland and that the present government was firmly established. The United States, he remarked, had waited until 1933 to recognize the Soviet Government and would probably take just as long to recognize the Chinese.

After their first display of hurt feelings that Mr. Pearson should have attacked the Soviet Union unjustly, they did not return to the subject except in an occasional aside which showed that his remarks were still rankling. I was at a disadvantage in not knowing any more of what the Minister had said than was printed in *Pravda*.

The 20th Communist Party Congress and Watkins' Return to Ottawa,

February to April, 1956

The following despatches, detailing the climactic Twentieth Communist Party Congress of February, 1956, represent the dénouement of Watkins' Moscow posting. The Congress concluded with the now-famous speech by Khrushchev to a closed session, in which he attacked Stalin for his ruthlessness, irrationality and misjudgments. Specifically, Khrushchev railed at Stalin's purges of the party and the army in the 1930s, and blamed him for military unpreparedness during the Second World War. All this, Khrushchev said, was due to the "cult of personality," implying that with the death of the man himself, the old era had passed away as well. In fact, the denunciation caused disruptions within the Communist party at home and abroad, and tarnished all members of the Politburo who had worked under Stalin without challenging him — including Khrushchev himself.

— February 16, 1956 (Despatch 119) —

... The Congress was opened by Comrade N.S. Khrushchev, First Secretary of the Party, who proceeded to address the assembly for a little over seven hours without showing, I am assured, the slightest sign of fatigue. His speech was broadcast and listeners who heard the end of it said that his voice sounded as fresh and vigorous as if he were just beginning.

One's first impression on reading the document through is that Stalin is indeed dead, as Mr. Khrushchev pointed out before beginning his report and noted again in the course of it, and that, in the words of a Gilbert and Sullivan character, it *does* make a difference, doesn't it? "Shortly after the Nineteenth Congress, death took Joseph Vissarion-ovich Stalin from our ranks," Mr. Khrushchev says on page 148, and goes on immediately to boast that the confusion and discord in the Party's ranks for which the enemies of socialism were hoping failed to materialize. Instead, the Party rallied still more closely around its Central Committee and resolutely put an end to the criminal conspiracy of that dangerous enemy on whom the imperialists had placed special hopes "their old agent, Beria, who had perfidiously wormed his way into leading posts in the Party and Government." There is no tribute to Stalin after the formal gesture of standing up at the beginning to mark his passing ... There are several references to Marxism-Leninism but none to Marxism-Leninism-Stalinism. One recalls what Khrushchev is reported to have said when he was in Yugoslavia: that for several months before Stalin's death he went around in terror of his life, especially after Stalin had called him to inquire whether or not the rumour that he had Jewish blood was true....

Mr. Khrushchev then attacks Stalin without naming him in a strong endorsement of "the Leninist principle of collective leadership." If Party unity was to be further consolidated, "it was necessary to re-establish the Party standards worked out by Lenin, which in the past had frequently been violated." The Central Committee "vigorously condemned the cult of the individual as being alien to the spirit of Marxism-Leninism and making a particular leader a hero and miracle worker." In the words of the Party anthem, the "Internationale," he says, "we want no condescending saviours." Application of the Leninist principles in Party affairs, he continues, has heightened the activity of Party organizations, strengthened their ties with the working people, increased their influence among the masses. But he warns that even today, when the strength and prestige of the Party are higher than ever, they must not indulge in complacency and above all must raise the level of the Party's organizational and ideological activities....

And again Stalin is criticized without being named, since he was almost certainly the author of the *Short History* of the C.P.S.U. [Communist Party of the Soviet Union] ... on which for the past 17 years, Mr. Khrushchev says, their propaganda was principally based, and which should now be replaced by a popular text-book on Party history based on historical facts! Two other text-books are required; one setting out the cardinal principles of Marxist-Leninist theory in concise, simple and lucid language; and one giving a popular exposition of the fundamentals of Marxist philosophy. It may be that Mr. Khrushchev has literary ambitions.

— February 24, 1956 (Letter 142) —

[Watkins, Alyosha and two others had dinner at Anatoly's apartment.]

... When I said that I was weary from reading endless speeches [from the Party Congress], Alyosha thought I was getting off easy. He had had to sit through all of them and that was infinitely more tiring. Moreover, he had to leave the house every morning by 7 o'clock and usually got home again around midnight. In addition to that, he was starving, for he had not anything to eat since the night before. This was no doubt an exaggeration, for one can be sure that they all consume plenty of refreshments, both solid and liquid, from the buffets in the corridors.

Which of the speeches had I read? Mr. Khrushchev's, of course, which I had found the most interesting. They emphatically agreed, and Alyosha modestly said that it was very pleasant for him to hear me say so, because, as I might have guessed, he had drafted a good deal of it himself. (This seems to settle a point on which I was uncertain — that it is Mr. Khrushchev rather than Mr. Bulganin he works for.)

....

— **March 13, 1956 (Despatch 195)** —

[At a reception given by the French ambassador, Watkins spoke with Ralph Parker, the correspondent for the London *Daily Worker* who was soon to break the story of Khrushchev's secret denunciation of Stalin at the 20th Party Congress. Here Parker passes on to Watkins word of the Khrushchev speech. Parker is briefly described in the first despatch in this collection (Dec. 10, 1948).]

... As I have mentioned before, he [Parker] always makes a point, in order to improve his social position, I suppose, of trying to impart some new information. This time he started off at once *in medias res*. The correspondents were all agog about a rumour that on the last day of the 20th Congress, in a closed session, at which all of the Soviet delegates were present but from which the foreign guests and the press were excluded, Mr. Khrushchev had delivered a speech lasting more than two hours in which he had criticized Stalin much more severely than Mr. Mikoyan, for instance, had done. He had even attacked his war record and accused him of causing unnecessary casualties. He [Stalin] had failed to act upon the warnings sent by Churchill and Roosevelt of a German attack and as a result the Russians were not as well prepared for it as they could have been. At one point in the Battle of Stalingrad, Khrushchev had telephoned from there to report that they had no guns. He got Malenkov on the wire but demanded to speak to Stalin personally. Although Stalin was standing only three feet away from Malenkov, he refused to speak to Khrushchev and Malenkov had had to say that he was not there.

Stalin had put himself above the Party and governed despotically instead of through the Council. His treatment of his colleagues had been scandalous. When they were called in to talk to him, they said good-bye to their families before they went. Mr. Khrushchev had gone into detail on such subjects as the falsification of documents (he read out Lenin's Will, which has never been published, in the course of his speech), on the notorious doctors' case, etc.

— March 22, 1956 (Despatch 214) —

Although censorship has been lifted on stories going abroad regarding Mr. Khrushchev's speech to the special session of the 20th Congress, and the account published by the London *Daily Worker* substantially confirms the rumours that have been flying about Moscow for the last fortnight, the Soviet press continues to ignore the subject. Meanwhile it seems evident that indoctrination of Party members is being carried on ... and it is understood a circular was sent out shortly after the conclusion of the Congress giving four examples of what had been meant by the references in the speeches to the harm caused by the "cult of personality." These are said to be:

a) The brutality of the collectivization programme. Collectivization itself was necessary, but the methods employed were not, and were Stalin's responsibility.
b) The purges. Not only did Stalin frequently act without the advice or knowledge of his colleagues, but the form taken by the charges [was] frequently false ... and the purges of the Army left Russia in a weak position to face a German attack.
c) Poor military leadership. The example cited is said to be the unnecessary losses incurred in the Kharkov campaign.
d) The "Doctors' Plot," which is revealed as a pure fabrication of Stalin's.

So far as the general public is concerned, the deflation of Stalin is being handled fairly cautiously, and there has been no wholesale purging of images. The main physical indication recently of what is going on was the taking down of most of Stalin's portraits from the Tretyakov Gallery. The change is reflected in other ways, however. I visited the Revolutionary Museum for the first time a few days ago, and Stalin is certainly very much in evidence there, although for the most part in paintings showing him at Lenin's side. Where the change comes is in the lectures of the guide. I noticed that references to Stalin seemed to be deliberately avoided, and a member of the American Embassy heard a guide point out that there was a slight historical inaccuracy in the picture of Lenin addressing the crowd at the Finland Station: Stalin had not been there.

— **April 15, 1956 (Despatch 268)** —

[In early April, Watkins learned he was being recalled to Canada to become assistant undersecretary. The following is one of his last communications with Ottawa before departing.]

I should have commented before now on Mr. [R.A.D.] Ford's very interesting and comprehensive paper on the destruction of the Stalin myth, with whose conclusions I generally agree, but have, I am afraid, allowed myself to be diverted from more important tasks by the inevitable round of farewell calls and hospitality....

One of the reasons for using the 20th Congress to criticize Stalin so severely is said by Russians to be the need to encourage individual initiative and responsibility at many levels in order to advance industrial and agricultural production more rapidly. Under Stalin, they say, the country was paralyzed. Many people with valuable ideas were simply afraid to put them forward because of what happened to persons accused of propagating erroneous views....

... One senses in the Russia of the 20th Congress a consciousness that the Soviet Union is emerging from a long, hard period of struggle and is now facing up to the resultant responsibilities as well as opportunities. Amongst the responsibilities is the very real problem of dealing, for the first time in Russian history, with a largely literate population and an increasingly important elite in the bureaucracy, universities, institutes, research organizations and so on who could hardly be expected to pay more than cynical lip-service in the long run to the more obvious distortions and omissions of the official version of Soviet history. To retain their respect and loyalty the Party no doubt realized that a more objective (in the Western sense) approach had to be introduced, and this could hardly be done without dismantling a large part of the intellectual scaffolding erected by Stalin. The degree of objectivity must have been, and must still be, a delicate question for the party leaders to resolve. To appear genuinely objective the attack on Stalin himself must be kept within bounds, and not become a personal vendetta as irrational as the myth itself....

... One of the things that has impressed me most during my stay here has been the evidence of extreme social mobility resulting from the Soviet educational system, and the way it is taken for granted by, say, a taxi driver that his sons will become members of the scientific or artistic middle class, and may even join the elite if they can qualify for this status. This in turn reflects the increasing demand for technical and managerial personnel, and their increasing importance in the political economy of Russia....

With reference to ... the significance of the destruction of the Stalin myth in the international field ... my own inclination would be to regard this as very much a secondary consideration in the minds of the Soviet leaders. Cutting Stalin down to size may pay incidental dividends in making communism more respectable abroad (and I agree that, generally speaking, a post-revolutionary hankering after respectability is increasingly important), but ... this is balanced in the short run at least by confusion in the party ranks and by the ridiculous posture in which the more ardent foreign apologists are now left. Some responsible foreign observers here think that even Khrushchev may have lost some stature in the eyes of many Russians by revealing the abject servility of the top Party figures during the last dark days in the Kremlin. I doubt myself whether given Russian mentality and tradition, this is really the case; but even if it is, they at least had a very good excuse.

John Watkins had one more overseas posting before he retired, but it is his Moscow despatches which will be long remembered. Watkins' curiosity for the passions, fears and prejudices of all he met, as well as his gift for words, bring his despatches to life more than three decades after they were put into the diplomatic bag bound for Ottawa. John Watkins captured something ageless in the Russian spirit, and what he divined in his Moscow postings may help to pierce the enigma of the Soviet Union today.

Notes

Chargé d'affaires

[1] *Russia is No Riddle* (New York, 1945); Stevens later produced an equally unremarkable study of post-war Soviet society, *This is Russia, Uncensored* (New York, [1950]).

[2] Ministerstvo Vnutrennykh Del, or Ministry for Internal Affairs, the Soviet secret police. On March 13, 1954 — ten days after Watkins' arrival in Moscow — secret police operations were formally reorganized under the new KGB. The MVD was reduced to conventional policing and firefighting, while the KGB took charge of running intelligence operations abroad, as well as internal political policing and blackmail operations against foreign diplomats in the Soviet Union. Watkins, like other Western diplomats and officials of the period, continued to refer to the MVD as the secret police apparently oblivious to the unannounced change in responsibilities.

Ambassador

[1] Gromyko is currently (1987) President of the U.S.S.R.

Interlude

[1] New Economic Policy. Begun by Lenin in 1921, the NEP allowed a measure of private enterprise in industry and agriculture.

Getting to know Anatoly and Alyosha

[1] The Communist Party of Canada was banned under the War Measures Act, and reconstituted itself during the Second World War as the Labour-Progressive Party.

[2] Watkins at this point earned $10,000 annually.

A visit by the Minister for External Affairs

[1] The aristocratic Yussupov family is perhaps best known for Prince Felix Yussupov who, in 1916, murdered Rasputin, the domineering spiritual adviser to the Czarina.

[2] General Alexis Ignatieff, a cousin of George's father, began his career under the czars. He is credited with rousing Soviet troops during the Nazi attack on Russia.

[3] Ignatieff reports that Alyosha used his first name only in conversation with him.

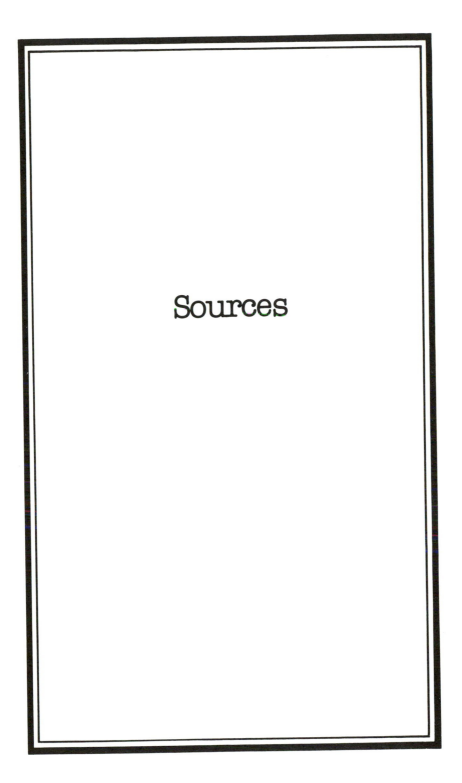

Sources

The following published sources were consulted in the preparation of this book:

Ian Adams, *S: Portrait of a Spy* (second edition, 1981); Aloysius Balawyder, *Canadian-Soviet Relations between the World Wars* (1972); John Barron, *KGB: The Secret Work of Secret Agents* (1974); Elizabeth Bentley, *Out of Bondage* (1951); Charles E. Bohlen, *Witness to History 1929-1969* (1973); Marshall Crowe and Arthur Blanchette, "John Watkins: An Appreciation," *International Perspectives*, vol. 10 (November-December, 1981), 32; James Eayrs, *Canada in World Affairs, October 1955 to June 1957* (1959); Anatoly Golitsyn, *New Lies for Old* (1984); Sir William Hayter, *The Kremlin and the Embassy* (1966); John W. Holmes, *The Shaping of the Peace: Canada and the Search for World Order, 1943-1957*, vol. 2, (1982); George Ignatieff, *The Making of a Peacemonger* (1985); Lydia Kirk, *Postmarked Moscow* (1952); René Levesque, *Memoirs*, trans. by Philip Stratford (1986); Boris Levytsky, *The Uses of Terror: The Soviet Secret Service 1917-1970* (1971); Carl H. McMillan, *Canada's Postwar Economic Relations with the U.S.S.R.: An Appraisal* (1979); David Martin, *Wilderness of Mirrors* (1980); Donald C. Masters, *Canada in World Affairs, 1953 to 1955* (1959); John A. Munro and Alex I. Inglis, eds., *Mike: The Memoirs of the Right Honourable Lester B. Pearson*, vol. 2, (1973); Albert Parry, "Russia's New Look at Canada," *Queen's Quarterly*, vol. 64, no. 1 (spring, 1957), 27-40; Chapman Pincher, *Their Trade is Treachery* (1981) and *Too Secret Too Long* (1984); Charles Ritchie, *Storm Signals: More Undiplomatic Diaries, 1962-1971* (1983); John Sawatsky, *Men in the Shadows: The RCMP Security Service* (1980) and *For Services Rendered: Leslie James Bennett and the RCMP Security Service* (1983); Robert A. Spencer, *Canada in World Affairs, from UN to NATO, 1946-1949* (1959); Dana Wilgress, *Memoirs* (1967) and "From Siberia to Kuibyshev: Reflections on Russia, 1919-1943," *International Journal*, vol. 22, no. 3 (summer 1967), 364-375; Reginald Whitaker, "Origins of the Canadian government's internal security system, 1946-1952," *Canadian Historical Review*, vol 65, no. 2 (June 1984), 154-183. Press clippings, 1948-1982: The Canadian Press, Kingston *Whig-Standard*, Montreal *Gazette*, Ottawa *Citizen*, Toronto *Globe and Mail*, Toronto *Star*, Toronto *Sun*, Vancouver *Sun*, Winnipeg *Free Press*. Hansard.

Also consulted were the following archival materials:

Transcript of the 1981-82 Quebec coroner's inquest into the death of John Watkins (several key exhibits have disappeared without explanation); personnel file on John Watkins compiled by the Department of External Affairs (held by the Public Archives of Canada); FBI Watkins file; parts of the RCMP Security Service report of the Watkins interrogation; letters by Watkins to friends and associates.

All research materials related to this book are being deposited with the University of Toronto archives; specific queries about sources can be relayed to the authors through the publisher.